CAE Specification

Data Storage Management — A Systems Approach

The Open Group

/

The Open Group and Prentice Hall are pleased to join forces to make available some of The Open Group's key works. This title is especially selected by The Open Group and Prentice Hall for distribution through the international book trade by Prentice Hall.

Prentice Hall ISBN: 0-13-890187-2

Equivalent X/Open Document:

CAE Specification

Systems Management: Data Storage Management (XDSM) API

ISBN: 1-85912-190-X
Document Number: C429

Published in the U.K. by The Open Group, February 1997.

Any comments relating to the material contained in this document may be submitted to:

The Open Group
Apex Plaza
Forbury Road
Reading
Berkshire, RG1 1AX
United Kingdom

or by Electronic Mail to:

OGSpecs@opengroup.org

Contents

List of Figures

List of Tables

Preface

The Open Group

The Open Group is an international open systems organisation that is leading the way in creating the infrastructure needed for the development of network-centric computing and the information superhighway. Formed in 1996 by the merger of the X/Open Company and the Open Software Foundation, The Open Group is supported by most of the world's largest user organisations, information systems vendors and software suppliers. By combining the strengths of open systems specifications and a proven branding scheme with collaborative technology development and advanced research, The Open Group is well positioned to assist user organisations, vendors and suppliers in the development and implementation of products supporting the adoption and proliferation of open systems.

With more than 300 member companies, The Open Group helps the IT industry to advance technologically while managing the change caused by innovation. It does this by:

- consolidating, prioritising and communicating customer requirements to vendors
- conducting research and development with industry, academia and government agencies to deliver innovation and economy through projects associated with its Research Institute
- managing cost-effective development efforts that accelerate consistent multi-vendor deployment of technology in response to customer requirements
- adopting, integrating and publishing industry standard specifications that provide an essential set of blueprints for building open information systems and integrating new technology as it becomes available
- licensing and promoting the X/Open brand that designates vendor products which conform to X/Open Product Standards
- promoting the benefits of open systems to customers, vendors and the public.

The Open Group operates in all phases of the open systems technology lifecycle including innovation, market adoption, product development and proliferation. Presently, it focuses on seven strategic areas: open systems application platform development, architecture, distributed systems management, interoperability, distributed computing environment, security, and the information superhighway. The Open Group is also responsible for the management of the UNIX trade mark on behalf of the industry.

The X/Open Process

This description is used to cover the whole Process developed and evolved by X/Open. It includes the identification of requirements for open systems, development of CAE and Preliminary Specifications through an industry consensus review and adoption procedure (in parallel with formal standards work), and the development of tests and conformance criteria.

This leads to the preparation of a Product Standard which is the name used for the documentation that records the conformance requirements (and other information) to which a vendor may register a product. There are currently two forms of Product Standard, namely the Profile Definition and the Component Definition, although these will eventually be merged into one.

The X/Open brand logo is used by vendors to demonstrate that their products conform to the relevant Product Standard. By use of the X/Open brand they guarantee, through the X/Open Trade Mark Licence Agreement (TMLA), to maintain their products in conformance with the Product Standard so that the product works, will continue to work, and that any problems will be fixed by the vendor.

Open Group Publications

The Open Group publishes a wide range of technical literature, the main part of which is focused on specification development and product documentation, but which also includes Guides, Snapshots, Technical Studies, Branding and Testing documentation, industry surveys and business titles.

There are several types of specification:

- *CAE Specifications*

  CAE (Common Applications Environment) Specifications are the stable specifications that form the basis for our product standards, which are used to develop X/Open branded systems. These specifications are intended to be used widely within the industry for product development and procurement purposes.

  Anyone developing products that implement a CAE Specification can enjoy the benefits of a single, widely supported industry standard. In addition, they can demonstrate product compliance through the X/Open brand. CAE Specifications are published as soon as they are developed, so enabling vendors to proceed with development of conformant products without delay.

- *Preliminary Specifications*

  Preliminary Specifications usually address an emerging area of technology and consequently are not yet supported by multiple sources of stable conformant implementations. They are published for the purpose of validation through implementation of products. A Preliminary Specification is not a draft specification; rather, it is as stable as can be achieved, through applying The Open Group's rigorous development and review procedures.

  Preliminary Specifications are analogous to the *trial-use* standards issued by formal standards organisations, and developers are encouraged to develop products on the basis of them. However, experience through implementation work may result in significant (possibly upwardly incompatible) changes before its progression to becoming a CAE Specification. While the intent is to progress Preliminary Specifications to corresponding CAE Specifications, the ability to do so depends on consensus among Open Group members.

- *Consortium and Technology Specifications*

  The Open Group publishes specifications on behalf of industry consortia. For example, it publishes the NMF SPIRIT procurement specifications on behalf of the Network Management Forum. It also publishes Technology Specifications relating to OSF/1, DCE, OSF/Motif and CDE.

  Technology Specifications (formerly AES Specifications) are often candidates for consensus review, and may be adopted as CAE Specifications, in which case the relevant Technology Specification is superseded by a CAE Specification.

In addition, The Open Group publishes:

- *Product Documentation*

  This includes product documentation — programmer's guides, user manuals, and so on — relating to the Pre-structured Technology Projects (PSTs), such as DCE and CDE. It also includes the Single UNIX Documentation, designed for use as common product documentation for the whole industry.

- *Guides*

  These provide information that is useful in the evaluation, procurement, development or management of open systems, particularly those that relate to the CAE Specifications. The Open Group Guides are advisory, not normative, and should not be referenced for purposes of specifying or claiming conformance to a Product Standard.

- *Technical Studies*

  Technical Studies present results of analyses performed on subjects of interest in areas relevant to The Open Group's Technical Programme. They are intended to communicate the findings to the outside world so as to stimulate discussion and activity in other bodies and the industry in general.

- *Snapshots*

  These provide a mechanism to disseminate information on its current direction and thinking, in advance of possible development of a Specification, Guide or Technical Study. The intention is to stimulate industry debate and prototyping, and solicit feedback. A Snapshot represents the interim results of a technical activity.

Versions and Issues of Specifications

As with all *live* documents, CAE Specifications require revision to align with new developments and associated international standards. To distinguish between revised specifications which are fully backwards compatible and those which are not:

- A new *Version* indicates there is no change to the definitive information contained in the previous publication of that title, but additions/extensions are included. As such, it *replaces* the previous publication.

- A new *Issue* indicates there is substantive change to the definitive information contained in the previous publication of that title, and there may also be additions/extensions. As such, both previous and new documents are maintained as current publications.

Corrigenda

Readers should note that Corrigenda may apply to any publication. Corrigenda information is published on the World-Wide Web at **http://www.opengroup.org/public/pubs**.

Ordering Information

Full catalogue and ordering information on all Open Group publications is available on the World-Wide Web at **http://www.opengroup.org/public/pubs**.

This Document

This Data Storage Management (XDSM) API is a CAE Specification. It defines APIs which use events to notify Data Management (DM) applications about operations on files, enable DM applications to store arbitrary attribute information with a file, support managed regions within a file, and use DMAPI access rights to control access to a file object. DMAPI refers to the interface defined by this XDSM Specification.

To adequately support data management applications, a file system and its host Operating System must include a set of functions and semantics not found in most POSIX-compliant systems. These extensions include the capability to monitor events on files, and special interfaces to manage and maintain the data in a file.

Data management applications such as file backup and recovery, file migration, and file replication, typically function as logical extensions of the Operating System. They often must have special permissions (such as ''root'' or file system credentials) to operate. The interfaces and data structures described in this document are all designed for these specific applications. These interfaces are not intended for direct use by typical end-users or unprivileged processes.

Intended Audience

This document is intended for developers writing Data Management API-compliant applications, or implementing the XDSM API in an operating system.

It is assumed the reader has a good understanding of standard UNIX semantics, is familiar with the C language, and understands the issues and tradeoffs in writing data management software.

Structure

This specification is organized as follows:

- Chapter 1 provides a high-level overview of the features and functionality of the XDSM API.
- Chapter 2 outlines the specific interfaces and describes their use.
- Chapter 3 covers the event messages.
- Chapter 4 describes the DMAPI data structures.
- Chapter 5 contains man-page definitions for the API function calls.
- Chapter 6 provides implementation notes intended to highlight subtle or complex areas of the DMAPI definition.

Typographical Conventions

The following typographical conventions are used throughout this document:

- **Bold** font is used in text for filenames, keywords, type names, data structures and their members.
- *Italic* strings are used for emphasis or to identify the first instance of a word requiring definition. Italics in text also denote:
  - — variable names, for example, substitutable argument prototypes, parameters and environment variables
  - — options in text
  - — C-language functions; these are shown as follows: *name*()

- Normal font is used for the names of constants and literals.
- The notation **<file.h>** indicates a C-language header file.
- The notation [ABCD] is used to identify a coded return value in C.
- Syntax and C-code examples are shown in `fixed width` font.

Trade Marks

Motif®, OSF/1® and UNIX® are registered trademarks and the ''X Device''™ and The Open Group™ are trademarks of The Open Group.

Referenced Documents

The following documents are referenced in this CAE Specification:

XSH, Issue 5
: CAE Specification, January 1997, System Interfaces and Headers, Issue 5 (ISBN: 1-85912-181-0, C606).

XCU, Issue 5
: CAE Specification, January 1997, Commands and Utilities, Issue 5 (ISBN: 1-85912-191-8, C604).

XBD, Issue 5
: CAE Specification, January 1997, System Interface Definitions, Issue 5 (ISBN: 1-85912-186-1, C605).

Curses Interface, Issue 5
: CAE Specification, May 1996, X/Open Curses, Issue 4, Version 2 (ISBN: 1-85912-171-3, C610), plus Corrigendum U018.

XNS, Issue 5
: CAE Specification, February 1997, Networking Services, Issue 5 (ISBN: 1-85912-165-9, C523).

Chapter 1

Overview

1.1 Scope and Purpose

To adequately support data management applications, a file system and its host Operating System must include a set of functions and semantics not found in most POSIX-compliant systems. These extensions include the capability to monitor events on files and special interfaces to manage and maintain the data in a file.

The important features of the DMAPI as described in this document are the use of events to notify DM applications about operations on files, the ability of DM applications to store arbitrary attribute information with a file, support for managed regions within a file, and the use of DMAPI access rights to control access to a file object.

Data management applications such as file backup and recovery, file migration, and file replication typically function as logical extensions of the operating system. They often must have special permissions (such as root or file system credentials) to operate. The interfaces and data structures described in this document are all designed for these specific applications. These interfaces are not intended for direct use by typical end-users or unprivileged processes.

1.2 Events

Events and managed regions are the foundations of the DMAPI. In the event paradigm, the operating system informs a DM application running in user space when a particular event occurs. For example, a DM application in user space can request that it be notified whenever a read of a certain area of a file occurs. When the operating system determines that it is going to read data from the target area, it notifies the DM application via a DMAPI event. In this manner, DM applications can monitor and manage files and specific regions within those files.

Files can be divided into distinct portions known as managed regions. Some types of DMAPI events are produced on a per region basis; this allows for finer granularity of event notification and reduces the number of messages between the operating system and the DM application.

1.2.1 Tokens

One of the fundamental concepts of the DMAPI is that of a token. A token is a reference to state associated with a synchronous event message. This state may include lists of files affected by the event, the access rights that are currently in force for those files, and so forth. The token provides DM applications with a simple method of referencing this state. Most DMAPI functions require a token as one of their parameters.

1.2.2 Access Rights

The DMAPI provides DM applications with the ability to control access to a file object. There are three forms of access rights: DM_RIGHT_NULL, DM_RIGHT_SHARED, and DM_RIGHT_EXCL. These rights are mutually exclusive; it is not possible to have a DM_RIGHT_SHARED right in effect on an object at the same time as a DM_RIGHT_EXCL right.

A DM_RIGHT_SHARED right grants its holder the right to read or query a file system object; this is called a shared right. A DM_RIGHT_EXCL right grants its holder all of the DM_RIGHT_SHARED rights plus the right to modify a file system object; this is called an exclusive right. As the names suggest, there may be multiple DM_RIGHT_SHARED rights granted on an object at one time. There can be only one DM_RIGHT_EXCL right granted, and it excludes DM_RIGHT_SHARED rights as well.

Access rights to a file system object may be conveyed to a DM application as part of sending a synchronous event message. DM applications must use the *dm_query_right*( ), *dm_request_right*( ), and *dm_release_right*( ) interfaces to determine the access rights that have been conveyed.

DMAPI access rights provide a mechanism for a DM application to synchronize accesses by other processes. If a token references an outstanding message that conveys the DM_RIGHT_EXCL access right for a file, then only processes presenting that token as an argument to a DMAPI function may access the file; all other attempted accesses to the file (including from within the operating system) are blocked.

These access rights provide a level of abstraction from internal operating system locks. Each Operating System will have different locking requirements and implementations. Using the DMAPI access rights provides DM applications a consistent interface to the Operating System, regardless of the internal locking model.

For more information on access rights, tokens, and synchronous messages, see the Sessions and Event Messages, Tokens, and Access Rights sections.

1.3 Managed Regions

A managed region designates a specific portion of a file that is managed by a DM application. Managed regions allow exception events to be generated only for those parts of the file in which the DM application has interest.

A managed region consists of the following information:

- starting offset in the file
- length of the region
- a set of event flags.

Persistence, the duration of the period over which a given managed region exists, of this information is implementation specific, and can be determined through a DMAPI configuration function.

1.4 Handles

The DMAPI uses handles to identify file system objects. All of the interfaces in this document use handles as opposed to file descriptors. A special handle that references a file system as a whole is provided along with another one that allows receiving events when file systems are being mounted.

1.5 Sessions

The interface between the operating system and the DM application is session based. Sessions identify the recipient of an event message, and can also provide the DMAPI implementation with the ability to track, audit, and control the use of DMAPI facilities. Internally, sessions can be used by the DMAPI implementation as a mechanism to identify the queues that messages are placed on. Sessions are not persistent across reboots.

1.6 Data Management Attributes

DM applications typically use extended attributes to store pertinent information about a file. Attributes in this context are termed opaque since these attributes only have meaning to the application that created them. Non-opaque attributes provide information that is visible to the DMAPI implementation, such as managed region layout or event lists.

For example, the following are typical examples of opaque extended attributes:

- bitfile IDs
- location on secondary or tertiary storage
- indication that portions of the file are non-resident
- inheritable policy bits such as *lock on magnetic storage*.

Extended attributes accessed through the DMAPI are distinct from any extended attribute facility the underlying file system may happen to provide. (If available, the DMAPI implementation may choose to use such a facility to provide DMAPI attributes, but doing so is not required.)

The DMAPI provides mechanisms for storage of both opaque and non-opaque per-file attributes. Persistence of opaque attributes across reboots is a DMAPI implementation option. DM applications should use the *dm_get_config*( ) function to determine what the implementation provides.

1.7 Holes

Holes in a file can be created in two ways. First, as defined by POSIX 1003.1 - 1990:

> The *lseek*( ) function shall allow the file offset to be set beyond the end of existing data in the file. If data is later written at this point, subsequent reads of data in the gap shall return bytes with the value zero until data is actually written into the gap.

Holes can also be created by the *dm_punch_hole*( ) operation. It is the intent of this specification that a file system optimize the representation of holes so that large holes can be represented without consuming media resources. Most hierarchical-storage style DM application implicitly require the ability of a file system to represent at least one hole (covering the entire file) efficiently.

1.8 DMAPI Implementation Options

An implementation of the DMAPI may support optional components of this specification. The specifics of what optional components are implemented can be obtained by the *dm_get_config*( ) function. The *dm_get_config*( ) function returns, for a file system, whether the following optional functions are supported:

- the *dm_get_bulkall*( ) function
- *creation-by-handle* functions
- ''legacy'' handle functions
- non-blocking lock upgrades
- the *dm_pending*( ) function
- persistent, opaque attributes
- persistent event masks
- persistent inherited attributes
- persistent managed regions.

dm_get_config( ) also returns the implementation's limits on various functions:

- maximum number of bytes returned for the attribute copy with destroy events
- maximum size of persistent attributes, if supported
- maximum handle size, if known
- maximum number of managed regions per file
- maximum number of bytes in user created event messages.

If an implementation does not support an optional function, [ENOSYS] will be returned to any calls made.

The *dm_init_service*( ) function also returns vendor defined version information. This should contain additional information on the specific DMAPI implementation, such as platform, the supported DMAPI specification version, and a vendor version identifier. A DMAPI implementation should provide information on how to interpret the return value from *dm_init_service*( ).

Chapter 2

Interfaces

Many of the interfaces described in this Chapter accept and return variable length data structures. For example, *handles* are variable length. Event messages are also variable length. For detailed information on accessing individual elements within a data structure, refer to the Data Structures definitions (see Chapter 4).

2.1 Initialization

An application that needs to use the features and functionality of the DMAPI must first call an initialization function. This allows implementations of the DMAPI to perform internal initialization procedures before providing service to an application. The DMAPI specification allows undefined behavior if applications do not use the initialization call. Another purpose of this function is to return a DMAPI implementation specific version string which may be used to determine at run-time whether the DM application is running on the correct implementation.

The following function exists for initializing the DMAPI:

dm_init_service( )	perform implementation-defined initialization.

2.2 Handles

A *handle* is an opaque identifier for an entity manipulated by the DMAPI. There are three fundamental categories of handles; the *global handle*, *file system handles*, and *object handles*.

The *global handle* is a fixed constant of the implementation, and is used primarily in the *dm_set_disp*( ) call when setting event disposition for the *mount* event. There is exactly one global handle in any DMAPI implementation.

File system handles are used by many DMAPI functions to identify a file system. There is one file system handle per file system. They are persistent and unique over time (per host) to the extent that a given file system instance has a unique and persistent identity.

Object handles are the most common. These are the handles used to represent all types of file system objects. Object handles are persistent and unique over time (per host) to the extent that a given file system instance has a unique and persistent identity. They are governed by the following properties:

- A unique object handle shall exist for each object visible in the file system name space. Each object handle shall be unique within at least the context of a single host.
- A unique object handle shall exist for each file system object not visible in the name space, such as unlinked but still-open files.
- Object handles must meet the following specific requirements with regard to uniqueness:
  - Object handles shall remain valid across any number of system reboots as long as the corresponding file system object exists.
  - Object handles shall remain valid if the file object they identify is renamed within a file system.

— Object handles shall remain valid regardless of any operations on the file object they identify. The only time an object handle becomes invalid is when the object it identifies ceases to exist.

- Object handles may be reused.

Some interfaces can only operate on object handles representing a specific type of file system object. For example, *dm_write_invis*( ) can only be used to write to a regular file. When necessary to describe restricted forms of object handles, the terms *file handle*, *directory handle*, *symlink handle*, etc. are used in this document. The taxonomy of handle terminology is shown in the following diagram.

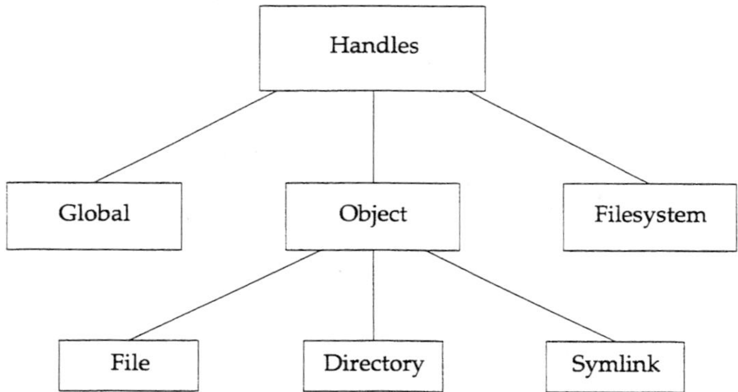

Figure 2-1 Taxonomy of Handles

Handles are opaque; the length of a handle is implementation defined. DM applications should make no assumptions about the length of a handle, as handles may be differing lengths even on the same file system in some DMAPI implementations. Therefore, functions that use handles in their interfaces specify two parameters: a *void* * that provides access to the actual handle, and a *size_t* that specifies the length of the handle. The DMAPI implementation allocates space for handles via the *dm_path_to_handle*( ), *dm_fd_to_handle*( ), and *dm_path_to_fshandle*( ) functions.

When a DM application is finished with the handle, it should free the space via the *dm_handle_free*( ) function.

Most DMAPI functions take a handle as part of their interface. Many events also provide a handle as part of their event-specific data. To convert from path names and file descriptors to handles, a number of functions are provided, as described in the man-pages. They are outlined below:

- *dm_path_to_handle*( )
  Create a file handle from a path name.

- *dm_fd_to_handle*( )
  Create a file handle from a file descriptor.

- *dm_path_to_fshandle*( )
  Create a file system handle from a path name.

- *dm_handle_cmp*( )
  File handle comparison.

- *dm_handle_free*( )
  Free the storage allocated for a handle.
- *dm_handle_is_valid*( )
  Determine if a handle is valid.
- *dm_handle_hash*( )
  Hashes the contents of a handle.

Some legacy DM applications rely on the fact that the DMAPI object handles are built from the combination of file system ID, file inode, and generation number. Such applications may require the capability to decompose DMAPI handles into these components and to build handles from these components.

The following **optional** interfaces are provided for this purpose:

- *dm_make_handle*( )
  Construct a DMAPI object handle.
- *dm_handle_to_fsid*( )
  Extract the file system ID from a handle.
- *dm_handle_to_igen*( )
  Extract the inode generation count from a handle.
- *dm_handle_to_ino*( )
  Extract the file inode number ID from a handle.
- *dm_make_fshandle*( )
  Construct a DMAPI file system handle.

2.3 Sessions

Sessions can be thought of as message queues. The implementation of the DMAPI enqueues messages on a session to make them available to a DM application. A DM application can also request the DMAPI implementation to enqueue an application defined message on a session. Sessions provide a mechanism for a DM application to receive events.

A unique ID is associated with each session. A session ID is of type *dm_sessid_t* and is used to identify the recipient of an event message. Session IDs are opaque to DM applications. Sessions are also the cornerstone of the recovery mechanism.

Sessions are governed by the following restrictions:

- Sessions are not persistent across reboots.
- Sessions are unique for as long as the system is up; they are not unique across reboots.
- Sessions must be explicitly destroyed. If a process exits or otherwise aborts without doing a *dm_destroy_session*( ), then the behavior of the session is dictated by the constraints in the Sessions and Event Messages section, below.
- A session is not tied to a process. Any process that has successfully executed *dm_init_service*( ) can use any valid session ID.
- Session IDs should not be interpreted as file descriptors. The underlying implementation may use file descriptors, but the DM application should make no assumptions about the implementation.

2.3.1 Session Instantiation

A session must be created via *dm_create_session*( ) before a DM application can communicate with the DMAPI. When a session is created, it is possible to specify a previous instantiation of a session that will then be assumed (taken over), which is useful for recovery purposes. The *dm_create_session*( ) function is atomic; if the call succeeds, the DMAPI guarantees that all old messages that were enqueued on the old session are now part of the new session. When assuming an existing session the old session is invalid when the call returns.

To shut down and destroy a session, a DM application may have to perform a number of operations, such as ensuring that no more events are generated, responding to outstanding messages, and so forth. If a DM application attempts to destroy a session that has outstanding event messages still enqueued, an error is returned. It is assumed that *dm_destroy_session*( ) will only be called after the application has ensured that no more events will be generated on the session.

The following functions are provided for manipulating an instantiation of a session:

- *dm_create_session*( )
  Create a new session; an old session may also be assumed.

- *dm_destroy_session*( )
  Destroy the specified session.

2.3.2 Sessions and Event Messages

At any time, a session may have synchronous event messages that are in one of two states:

- enqueued, undelivered

- delivered and awaiting a response from the DM application.

From the standpoint of the DMAPI implementation, synchronous event messages that are in the second state (delivered and awaiting a response) are outstanding. Asynchronous messages do not require a response from the DM application, and therefore will never be in the outstanding state.

In Figure 2-2, there are three event messages on the session. Each event message is identified by a unique token. One synchronous event message has been delivered to a DM application, and therefore the session has an outstanding message. The event message continues to exist until some DM application responds to it. The two other event messages on the session are just enqueued and have not yet been delivered to a DM application.

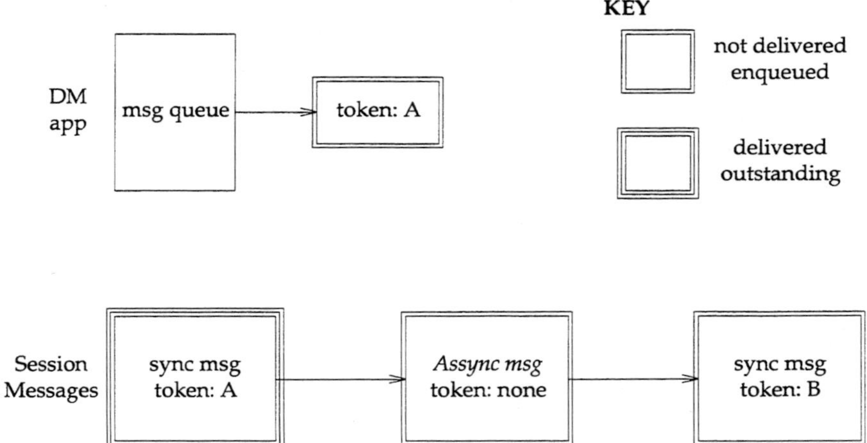

Figure 2-2 Message States

As part of sending a synchronous event message, the implementation of the DMAPI may convey access rights to one or more objects in the message. If a DM application fails (dies, hangs, or otherwise malfunctions), a recovery process must determine the outstanding event messages and take care of the associated events to prevent the system from hanging. Since tokens are tied to a session, and are always associated with a synchronous event message, it is possible to obtain all outstanding event messages simply by knowing all the tokens.

An active session is not needed to obtain the list of all valid sessions in the system. This allows a recovery application to interrogate all sessions even in the unlikely event the system runs out of sessions.

Recovering after a DM application failure is very different from recovering from a system crash. The requirements of each individual DM application will be unique with respect to recovery from a system crash; it is beyond the scope of the DMAPI to provide all the tools for a DM application to recover itself in this instance.

The following interfaces exist to manage session and event message recovery.

- *dm_getall_sessions*( )
  Obtain all valid sessions in the system.
- *dm_query_session*( )
  Retrieve the information associated with the session when it was created.
- *dm_getall_tokens*( )
  Get all tokens for all outstanding event messages for a session.
- *dm_find_eventmsg*( )
  Get the message for an event.

2.4 Tokens

Tokens are a reference to state associated with a synchronous event message. They are always associated with one and only one synchronous event message. When responding to an event message, the same token that was delivered with the message must be supplied. Tokens are the identifier that a DM application must use to reference a synchronous event message; the DM application presents the token to the DMAPI and in return, is provided with the state associated with the event message.

Like session IDs, tokens are opaque to DM applications. There is no security expressed or implied by the possession or use of a token. If a DM application can "guess" the value of a token, then it can use it (assuming that it can supply the appropriate session ID and has other system-dependent privileges).

Tokens have the following properties:

- Tokens are not owned by any particular process.
- The DMAPI does not mandate authentication or authorization of the process using the token; if a process knows a token's value, it can use it.
- Tokens are meaningful only within the session under which they were created unless a session is assumed from a previous session.

2.5 Access Rights

There are two primary rights; DM_RIGHT_SHARED and DM_RIGHT_EXCL. The third access right, DM_RIGHT_NULL, is not considered a primary access right, since it conveys no rights to an object.

Synchronous event messages contain access rights to one or more object handles. Some event messages contain multiple file handles. The event message contains access rights to all the files in the event message; the DM application must use *dm_query_right*( ) to determine what rights for the given file handles, if any, are present in the message.

If a DM application needs to obtain access rights for more than one handle, it can use the same token in repeated function calls to *dm_request_right*( ) and *dm_release_right*( ). It is not necessary for a new message (and its corresponding token) to be created via *dm_create_userevent*( ) for each handle the DM application needs to acquire access rights to.

As already noted, tokens do not belong to any particular process. An application presents a token to the DMAPI to reference and identify a specific access right. When a DM application is informally described as "holding a token" or "obtaining an access right", a more precise description would be that an outstanding access right exists, is encapsulated within a synchronous event message, is associated with a specific session, and is identified by a specific token.

Many DMAPI functions require a token that references a specific access right to an object. In some cases, it may be advantageous for a DM application not to have to go through the steps of explicitly creating a token and acquiring the necessary access rights just to call a DMAPI function. Therefore, many functions accept either a token that references the required rights, or the special value DM_NO_TOKEN, that indicates the absence of a token.

If a DM application does not pass a token to a DMAPI function that normally requires a token as one of its parameters, then the function acquires the appropriate rights automatically on behalf of the DM application. In this case, the DM application must be willing to be blocked. The DM application may or may not be blocked interruptibly, depending on the implementation of the

DMAPI; see the man-page definition for *dm_request_right*( ) for more information.

The DM application must use caution when availing itself of this optimization. If a DM application holds a token that references a right to an object, but fails to present it when calling a DMAPI function, then the application is in danger of deadlocking with itself. This is because the DMAPI function will not be able to acquire the necessary rights on behalf of the DM application since the application already holds a token referencing those rights. The DM application should also not use this method of acquiring access rights if it is receiving synchronous events via *dm_get_events*( ). Since one of the synchronous event messages may contain a token that references an access right the DM application may be trying to obtain, the application will again deadlock with itself.

The existence of any outstanding DM_RIGHT_SHARED access rights for a file system object will block all attempts from all processes performing the following operations:

- all data modification, such as via *write*(2)
- object destruction.

The existence of the DM_RIGHT_EXCL access right will block all attempts to perform any operation on the file system object, with the sole exception of the *stat*(2) family (*stat*, *lstat*, *fstat*, etc.).

The locking properties of access rights are summarized in the following table.

Access Right	**Blocked Operations**
DM_RIGHT_SHARED	data write, object destruction
DM_RIGHT_EXCL	all but *stat*(2)

Table 2-1 Access Right Properties for Files

Notice that the above descriptions do not say that other processes are blocked; they say that all processes are blocked. This is where the distinction that DM applications do not really "own" access rights comes into play.

The only way a DM application can distinguish itself from other processes that should be blocked is by knowing the **dm_token_t** value identifying the appropriate token, and passing it in with any operations that are to be performed on the file. It follows from this that once a DM application has "obtained" a DM_RIGHT_SHARED or DM_RIGHT_EXCL access right, either directly via a *dm_request_right*( ) call or indirectly via an event message, the DM application must be extremely cautious when performing operations on file system objects. Generally, it must restrict itself to using interfaces containing **dm_token_t** parameters.

For example, calling *dm_request_right*( ) and requesting DM_RIGHT_EXCL does not make a DM application the owner of the right; *dm_request_right*( ) merely creates the right and encapsulates it in the synchronous event message referenced by the token. Once that happens, all operations against the file system object will be blocked as described above, even if they come from the same process that called *dm_request_right*( ). Only operations that are part of the DMAPI and contain **dm_token_t** arguments are safe for DM application to call at this point, because those interfaces are the only way DM application can distinguish themselves as "owning" the DM_RIGHT_EXCL right.

2.5.1 Upgrading Access Rights

When requesting access rights to an object via *dm_request_right*( ), the requested right may not be immediately available. If the DM application has specified that it wants to block until the right becomes available, the DM app may or may not be blocked interruptibly. The implementation of the DMAPI will specify the semantics for interrupting blocked processes.

If a DM application holds a DM_RIGHT_SHARED access right, it can attempt to upgrade the right to a DM_RIGHT_EXCL in a non-blocking manner via *dm_request_right*( ). If the DMAPI implementation cannot grant the request, however, the DM application will most likely have to release the DM_RIGHT_SHARED right, and request DM_RIGHT_EXCL access to the object via *dm_request_right*( ) in a blocking fashion.

A DM application may also request to upgrade a DM_RIGHT_SHARED access right to a DM_RIGHT_EXCL in a non-blocking manner via *dm_upgrade_right*( ) if the DMAPI implementation is able to upgrade the right without releasing the DM_RIGHT_SHARED access right.

The state of the object cannot change while the DM application is waiting for an exclusive right via *dm_upgrade_right*( ). However, the state of the file may change if the request to upgrade is via *dm_request_right*( ). To provide some indication that the file changed while the application was blocked, the DMAPI provides the notion of a change indicator that can be interrogated via *dm_get_fileattr*( ). This change indicator is modified by any operation that modifies file data or metadata. The change indicator is not persistent and has no meaning across reboots. Its only purpose is to indicate to the DM application that the file may have changed since the last time the change indicator was interrogated.

The normal sequence of events for attempting a lock upgrade where the current shared lock must be dropped would be as follows:

1. Obtain current change indicator.
2. Release shared right.
3. Request exclusive right (blocking operation).
4. Obtain new change indicator to see if the file has changed.

The following functions for manipulating access rights are provided:

- *dm_downgrade_right*( )
  Downgrade an exclusive access right to a shared right.
- *dm_request_right*( )
  Request a specific access right to an object.
- *dm_release_right*( )
  Relinquish the access rights to an object.
- *dm_query_right*( )
  Determine the set of access rights to an object.
- *dm_upgrade_right*( )
  Upgrade a currently held access right to an exclusive right.

2.5.2 Placing Holds on Objects

If a DM application needs to make sure an object does not go away after releasing all access rights to the object, *dm_obj_ref_hold*( ) may be called to obtain an object hold. The effect is to prevent the object from being flushed out for the duration of the hold and essentially making non-persistent data management attributes temportarily persistent. Responding to an event releases all holds associated with the event.

The following functions are for manipulating object holds:

- *dm_obj_ref_hold*( )
  Place a hold on a file system object.
- *dm_obj_ref_rele*( )
  Release a hold on a file system object.
- *dm_obj_ref_query*( )
  Query for a hold on a file system object.

2.6 Finding Extents and Punching Holes

Data Management applications often need to release the on-disk blocks of a file to free up space on a file system. Likewise, if a large, but sparsely populated file is to be backed up efficiently, a DM application needs to know where the file has non-null data and where the file has holes. These operations may not be supported on all file system types; *dm_get_config*( ) can be used to determine if the underlying file system supports punching holes.

The DM application is responsible for maintaining accurate information about the location of any holes in the original file when a sparse file is made non-resident. It is assumed that the DM application will call *dm_get_allocinfo*( ) to determine where actual storage is located, and only perform *dm_read_invis*( ) operations on the portions of the file that contain data.

The following functions return information about a file in terms of a **dm_extent** structure, as defined in the Data Structures chapter (see Chapter 4). These functions, which do not affect any of a file's time stamps, are provided for managing the storage space for a file:

- *dm_get_allocinfo*( )
  Return the allocation information for the file specified by the handle.
- *dm_probe_hole*( )
  Interrogate the DMAPI implementation for size and offset around the area that the DM applications want to punch a hole.
- *dm_punch_hole*( )
  Logically write zeroes in the indicated region of the file identified by the handle, thereby allowing the DMAPI implementation to release media resources associated with that region. None of the file's time stamps are updated, but the file's DMAPI change indicator is updated.

2.7 Invisible Read and Write

Many data management applications must be able to access file data without altering the file's access, modification, and change times, and without generating any events. The operations in this section do not trigger events; they bypass the normal event delivery mechanism to prevent a DM application from receiving events generated by itself.

The invisible write function by default writes data asynchronously. If a DM application requires that data written to a file be flushed at certain times, it can either set a flag specifying that writes happen synchronously or it can call a separate function to flush the file's contents to media.

The following functions, which do not affect any of a file's time stamps, are provided:

- *dm_read_invis*( )
  Do a read without updating any of the file's time stamps.
- *dm_write_invis*( )
  Do a write without updating any of the file's time stamps. The DMAPI change indicator is updated. This function can execute synchronously or asynchronously.
- *dm_sync_by_handle*( )
  Synchronize a file's in-memory state with that on physical medium.

2.8 Managed Regions

Managed regions provide a mechanism for a data management application to control a specific region of a file. Managed regions provide granularity finer than the entire file for data events such as read and write. Their use is particularly important for very large files that may be larger than the actual amount of available disk space.

A single managed region is represented by a **dm_region** structure. The set of managed regions for a file is a collection of these structures. See Data Structures Chapter 4 for a definition of this structure.

The generation of events for a managed region is controlled by a flags field in the **dm_region** structure. The possible values for this field are a bitwise OR of one or more of the following:

DM_REGION_READ
: Generate a synchronous event for a read operation that overlaps this managed region.

DM_REGION_WRITE
: Generate a synchronous event for a write operation that overlaps this managed region.

DM_REGION_TRUNCATE Generate a synchronous event for a truncate operation that overlaps this managed region.

or the following value:

DM_REGION_NOEVENT
: Do not generate any events for this managed region.

The events defined above are the only synchronous data events that are defined for a managed region. Only one of the above events will be produced for a particular *read/write/truncate* operation, no matter how many managed regions the operation may overlap.

The example in Figure 2-3 below shows a read operation that overlaps two managed regions that have read events set.

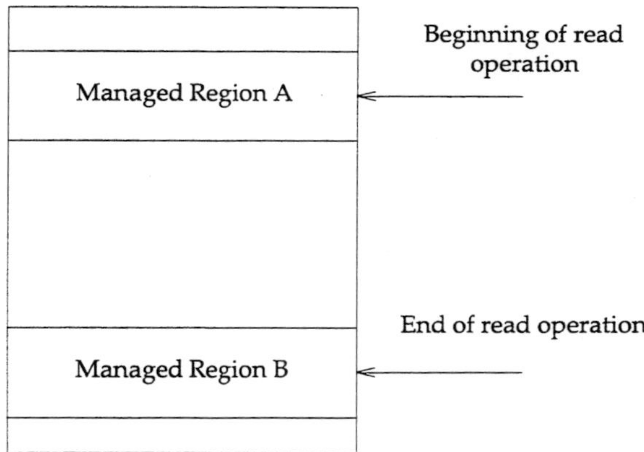

Figure 2-3 Overlapping of Events across Managed Regions

In Figure 2-3, a read event is produced for Managed Region A. The arguments passed to the DM application in the event message have the offset and length of the *read* operation; it is up to the DM application to determine which managed regions the operation will overlap. Once the DM application responds to the event message, the DMAPI implementation allows the read to continue.

As an example, if a DM application fills the managed region A above, but not B, and continues the operation, the behavior of the entire read operation is undefined.

Rationale:

Triggering one event per file operation eliminates the necessity of having the DMAPI implementation re-evaluate all managed regions involved in a given operation. Otherwise, the DMAPI implementation could be forced to generate multiple events per managed region for a single I/O operation.

To change the set of managed regions, the DM application must obtain DM_RIGHT_EXCL rights to the object. Since managed regions may or may not be persistent, the DM application must be prepared to expect a debut event and to use *dm_set_region*( ) to download the set of managed regions for a file.

Managed regions may be constrained by the following restrictions:

- Implementations may choose to support only one managed region per file, which may always be the entire file.
- Managed regions may not overlap. Each region is a distinct subset of the file.
- Only regular files may be partitioned into multiple managed regions.

A DM application can determine the properties of the DMAPI managed region implementation by consulting the *dm_get_config*( ) interface.

The following functions, which do not affect any of a file's time stamps, are provided for manipulating the managed regions of a file:

- *dm_get_region*( )
  Return the set of managed regions for a file.

- *dm_set_region*( )
  Set the managed regions for a file. The DMAPI change indicator is updated.

2.9 File Attributes and Bulk Retrieval

Attributes need to be retrieved for a single file, a directory, or a whole file system. The attributes returned are defined by the **dm_stat** structure. There are a number of methods for obtaining these file attributes:

- The *dm_get_fileattr*( ) function obtains the attributes for a single file specified by the file's handle.
- The attributes and names for all files in a directory can be obtained through use of the *dm_get_dirattrs*( ) function.
- The basic attributes for all files in a file system can be obtained through use of the *dm_get_bulkattr*( ) function.
- The basic attributes, plus a named DM attribute, for all files in a file system can be obtained through the use of the *dm_get_bulkall*( ) function.

For the second, third, and fourth methods, the application either provides a buffer large enough to contain all retrieved attributes or more commonly (particularly for the last option) the application makes iterative calls through the interface. A file system must be mounted to have its attributes retrieved via any of the above methods.

DM applications often need to set a file's metadata to specific values transparently. For example, a backup application might want to set a file's time stamps to their original value when the file is restored. Specific fields from the **dm_stat** structure are encapsulated in the **dm_fileattr** struct; this structure is used to set various metadata fields to specific values via *dm_set_fileattr*( ).

Before calling *dm_get_bulkattr*( ), *dm_get_dirattrs*( ), and *dm_get_bulkall*( ), the DM application must initialize an opaque "cookie" which provides location information to the DMAPI. Each call of *dm_get_bulkattr*( ), *dm_get_dirattrs*( ) or *dm_get_bulkall*( ) can use this cookie to determine location information from one call to the next.

The file's change indicator can also be retrieved using *dm_get_fileattr*( ). This change indicator is modified by any operation that modifies file data or metadata. DM applications can use the change indicator to determine if a file may have changed state; if the indicator is the same between two calls, the file is guaranteed not to have changed. If the indicator is different, the file may (but not necessarily) have changed. This is especially useful for attempting lock upgrades, as described in Upgrading Access Rights, Section 2.5.1 on page 12.

The following functions, which do not update any of an object's time stamps, are provided for obtaining bulk attributes:

- *dm_get_bulkall*( )
  Get the specified attributes in bulk for objects in a the given file system with a specific DM attribute.
- *dm_get_bulkattr*( )
  Get the specified attributes in bulk for the given file system.
- *dm_get_dirattrs*( )
  Get the specified file attributes and names in bulk for the given directory.
- *dm_init_attrloc*( )
  Initialize the location cookie for successive *dm_get_bulkattr*( ) calls.

The following function, which does not update any of a file's time stamps, is provided for obtaining the attributes of a single file:

- *dm_get_fileattr*( )
  Get the specified attributes for the given object.

The following function, which does not update any of the file's time stamps (other than those specified) as a side effect, is provided for metadata modification:

- *dm_set_fileattr*( )
  Set a specified attribute to a given value.

2.10 Data Management Attributes

Support for *persistent* data management attributes is a DMAPI implementation option. Some DMAPI implementations may not support persistent opaque data management attributes, while others may not provide support for persistent non-opaque attributes such as event lists. DM applications should use the *dm_get_config*( ) function to determine what the implementation provides.

A persistent attribute is one which stays defined across reboots. A non-persistent attribute is one that may disappear at any time without notice (typically during inode flush). For more information on how to manage non-persistent attributes, refer to the debut event.

2.10.1 Non-opaque Data Management Attributes

There are two types of non-opaque attributes:

- Managed Regions
  The DMAPI implementation may support persistence of managed regions. The *dm_get_config*( ) function returns the number of persistent managed regions supported.
- Event Bit Masks
  Event bit masks encode which events are enabled for a particular file within a finite number of persistent bits.

2.10.2 Opaque Data Management Attributes

The DMAPI persistent opaque attribute mechanism provides a set of (name, value) pairs associated with a file system object. The name is a fixed length 8 byte (defined as DM_ATTR_NAME_SIZE) opaque value determined by the DM application and is interpreted as a byte sequence. Attribute names starting with ASCII "_" (0x5F) are reserved for future common attribute labels. In order to prevent name clashes, the first three bytes of the attribute name are currently assigned through a reservation process. The prefix should identify the company whose DM product is using the attribute, for example, Cheyenne has "CYE" reserved.

> To register a 3-byte prefix, send e-mail to xdsmreg@xopen.org, identifying the company name and the requested name.

Registered prefixes can be checked on the World-Wide Web at the following location:

```
http://www.xopen.org/public/tech/sysman/xdsmreg.htm
```

The attribute value is variable length and also opaque. It is recommended that the values be stored in network byte order to support the movement of media between architectures. These attributes are persistent across reboots.

If the DM implementation supports opaque attributes, a limited number of attributes may be stored persistently with each file. Each attribute may store up to DM_CONFIG_MAX_ATTRIBUTE_SIZE bytes of data per file. The value of DM_CONFIG_MAX_ATTRIBUTE_SIZE is obtained via *dm_get_config*( ) and has a lower bound of 32 bytes. The total amount of space available for storage of all persistent attributes on a file system is bounded by DM_CONFIG_TOTAL_ATTRIBUTE_SPACE.

Associated with the file attributes is a per-file time stamp called *dtime*, which is updated when attributes are created, modified, or deleted, or when a new file inherits its attributes from the parent directory. The *dtime* time stamp may be the same as *ctime* as determined by the value returned from the *dm_get_config*( ) function with DM_CONFIG_DTIME_OVERLOADED. If *dtime* is not overloaded, then any operation that manipulates attributes does not modify the file's traditional time stamps (*atime*, *mtime*, *ctime*).

If DM_CONFIG_PERS_INHERIT_ATTRIBS (obtainable from *dm_get_config*( )) is DM_TRUE, DM applications can mark persistent attributes as inheritable. If a directory has an attribute (such as *lock_on_magnetic*) that has been marked inheritable and a file is created in the directory, then the file would inherit the attribute. Attributes that are not marked inheritable are not copied.

DM applications mark an attribute inheritable on a per-file system basis and for specified file types. For example, a DM application could mark the above attribute (*lock_on_magnetic*) inheritable for newly created regular files only. Newly-created directories would not inherit the attribute.

Attribute inheritance is not persistent across reboots. If a DM application marked the *lock_on_magnetic* attribute as inheritable and the system were then brought down, the attribute would no longer be inheritable when the system came back up.

The following functions are provided for attribute management:

- *dm_set_dmattr*( )
  Create a persistent attribute or override the contents of an existing attribute.
- *dm_getall_dmattr*( )
  Retrieve all of the DM attributes and their values for an object.
- *dm_get_dmattr*( )
  Retrieve the value of a specific attribute.
- *dm_remove_dmattr*( )
  Remove a specific attribute from an object.

The following functions are provided for managing inheritable attributes:

- *dm_set_inherit*( )
  Mark an attribute as inheritable on a file system.
- *dm_clear_inherit*( )
  Mark an attribute as no longer being inheritable.
- *dm_getall_inherit*( )
  Get all the attributes that have been marked inheritable on a file system. This is especially useful for application restart after a failure.

2.11 Events

The DMAPI provides DM applications with the ability to monitor and manage the data in a file system without having to export all the file system semantics from kernel space to user space via the event interface. Events are generated by a DMAPI implementation, and then the messages are enqueued on a session for delivery to a DM application.

The intent of the DMAPI is to support a single product on any single file system. The DMAPI does not preclude different products from different vendors operating on the same file system, but it is not recommended. Different products on different file systems are fully supported by the DMAPI with regard to event delivery.

Therefore, the following event restrictions exist:

- Multiple sessions cannot register disposition for the same event on the same object.
- Event messages are targeted to and enqueued on sessions; there is no explicit targeting of an event to a specific process.
- The behavior of event delivery when no session has requested to receive a particular event (that is, *dm_set_disp*( ) with the given event has not been executed) is DMAPI implementation-specific. The DMAPI implementation must document the behavior of the system and has one of these three choices:
  - — block the process that caused the event to be fired
  - — fail the operation
  - — not fire the event and allow the process to proceed as if there is no event disposition.

Certain events are optional in the DMAPI specification. It is recommended that for each file system being managed by a DM application, that the application initially call *dm_get_config_events*( ) to determine which events are supported by the DMAPI implementation for that file system.

- *dm_get_config_events*( )
  Get a list of all events supported by the DMAPI implementation

2.11.1 Setting Event Disposition

After creating a session, DM applications must register with the DMAPI to establish the disposition of events for a file system (that is, what session the events will be sent to). The event list is the complete set of all events, including managed region events, that the DM application is monitoring during the life of the session. Since registration is on a per-session basis, this event list is not persistent across reboots. It is not possible to register to receive events on anything other than the file system object.

Once a DM application has registered its event list and session with the DMAPI, it can begin receiving event messages on a file system. Registration can be thought of as establishing the association between a file system and a session, as it lets the DMAPI implementation know which session to send specific event messages to.

The example shown in Figure 2-4 illustrates the case where a DM application has registered with the file system represented by "foo" for the *read* and *write* events. The event messages are delivered to the application via session 42. The file *bar* has an event list of *read*, *write*, and *truncate* that was previously set via *dm_set_region*( ).

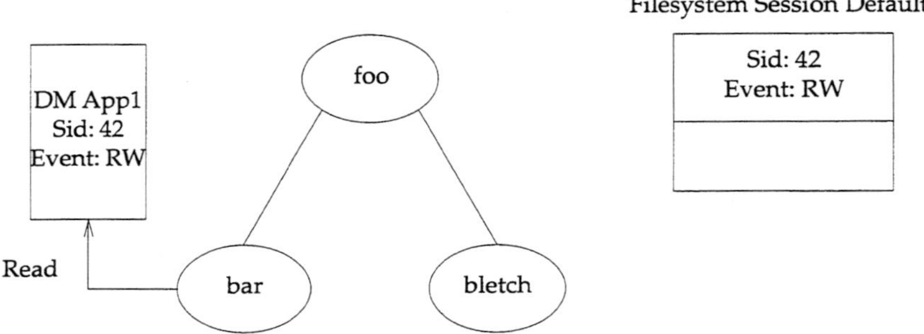

Figure 2-4 Disposition of Event Delivery

In Figure 2-4, the *read* event is delivered to DM application 1, since that is the session for that specific event.

Multiple applications can register their session and event list for a file system. If two applications attempt to register to receive the same event, the last application to register for the event will receive it; prior registrations for the event are replaced.

Rationale:

> If this were not the case, and replacement were done on an entire event list, not a per-event basis, then it would not be possible to have more than one active session registered for a file system. Having each event in the event list handled individually allows multiple applications to be active on the same file system simultaneously, all handling different events.

Figure 2-5 illustrates how Figure 2-4 would change if a second DM application registered for just the *read* events.

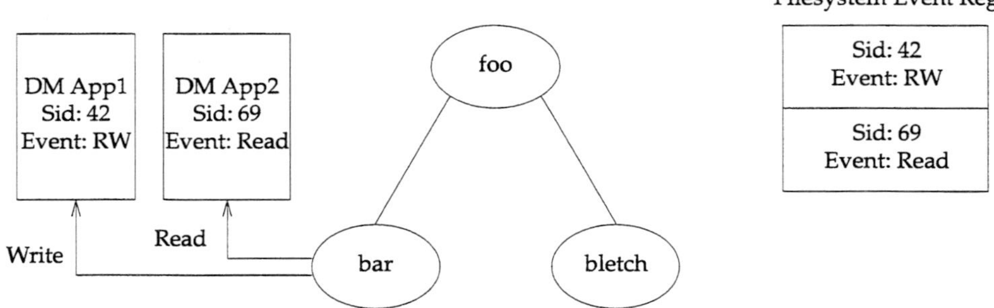

Figure 2-5 Duplicate Event Registrations on a File System

In Figure 2-5, *read* events are now sent to DM application 2, via session 69, not DM application 1. *write* events will still be delivered to DM application 1.

Rationale:

The burden is on the system administrator to ensure that two different DM applications do not attempt to control the same events on the same file system. In Figure 5, an alternative implementation of *dm_set_disp*( ) would be to return an error saying that an <event, file system, session> binding already exists. Another option would be to send a special event to DM app one, informing it that it no longer will be receiving *read* events. While these options could be implemented, it is believed that the level of complexity is not warranted for this version of the DMAPI.

The examples given above assume that the file system the DM application is monitoring is already mounted. However, it is quite possible that a DM application wants to set itself up to monitor a file system that is not yet mounted.

2.11.2 The "mount" Event

The restriction of only sending synchronous events to one session has special ramifications with regard to the *mount* event. It is not the intent of the DMAPI to force a model of one "super-daemon" that listens for mount events, and then forwards the event to the appropriate recipient. However, there is a special bootstrap problem with regard to receiving the *mount* event before a file system handle is available. To receive *mount* events, a DM application must use the global handle in the *dm_set_disp*( ) function. The *mount* event will be sent serially to each session that has executed *dm_set_disp*( ). The event is not broadcast to all sessions concurrently. The order in which the DMAPI implementation sends the event to the sessions is not defined.

The *mount* event will be sent for all file systems that support the DMAPI. Specifying the event in the *dm_set_eventlist*( ) function is not allowed, since the event is not persistent. When the *mount* event is received, the DM application can determine if it is interested in the file system that is specified in the event message. If a DM application is not interested in the file system, then it must respond to the event via *dm_respond_event*( ) with a code of DM_RESP_DONTCARE. The first DM application that responds to the event with DM_RESP_CONTINUE and an error code of zero prevents the event from being sent to any of the remaining sessions. If any DM application returns an error [DM_RESP_ABORT], then the *mount* event will not be sent to any other session.

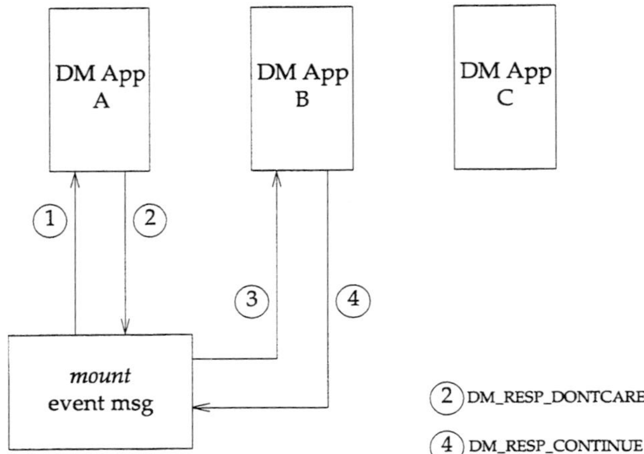

Figure 2-6 Mount Event Propagation

In Figure 2-6, 3 DM applications have specified via *dm_set_disp*( ) that they want to receive the *mount* event. The DMAPI implementation sends the *mount* event message to DM application A in step 1, which is not interested in the event, so it responds to the event message with DM_RESP_DONTCARE in step 2. The DMAPI implementation then sends the *mount* event message to DM application B in step 3, which determines that it wants to monitor the file system. It responds to the event message with a DM_RESP_CONTINUE in step 4, so the *mount* event is not sent to the remaining DM application C.

If all of the DM applications receiving *mount* events return DM_RESP_DONTCARE, then the file system *mount* proceeds normally.

For recovery processing, many DM applications will need the name of the file system device and the directory that it was mounted at. This information is made available via the *mount* event. During application restart, an application can get the same information via *dm_get_mountinfo*( ). A DM application would determine all the file systems that were being monitored via *dm_getall_disp*( ), and then use *dm_get_mountinfo*( ) to obtain more information about the file systems.

The following functions are provided for manipulating the disposition of a session's events for a file system:

- *dm_set_disp*( )
  Set the disposition of a session's events on a file system.
- *dm_getall_disp*( )
  Get the disposition of events for all file systems for a session.
- *dm_get_mountinfo*( )
  Get the information that was delivered on a *mount* event for the indicated file system.

2.11.3 Setting Event Notification

DM applications can specify that they need to receive certain events on an object. Events will only be generated for these objects, not for all objects in the file system (except for the *debut* event, discussed specifically later in this section). To set event notification on a object, the DM application must specify an event list for the object. This object is specified via a handle. The handle can be either the file system handle when setting events on a per file system basis, or a handle to a specific file system object. Executing *dm_set_eventlist*( ) may or may not persistently store the eventlist with the object; it is dependent on the particular implementation of the DMAPI. The persistence characteristic can be determined via the *dm_get_config*( ) function.

The DM application must specify the entire list of events that is to be generated for the object. If an event list already exists for the object, it is replaced by the new one specified in the *dm_set_eventlist*( ) function. If an event list was previously set for the entire file system, and a subsequent event list for an object in that file system includes an event that was set for the file system (or vice versa), the result is undefined. All events, with the exception of the managed region events and the *mount* event, can be specified in the *dm_set_eventlist*( ) function. If the object has multiple managed regions, then *dm_get_eventlist*( ) returns the union of all managed region events, in addition to the other events.

When an event is generated by the file system, the DMAPI implementation uses the session to determine the recipient. Since DM applications must register with the DMAPI via the *dm_set_disp*( ) to specify the event list and the session, the DMAPI can easily determine the target session for any given event.

Some implementations of the DMAPI may not provide any persistent storage, even for event notification. For these ''zero bit'' implementations, the DMAPI provides a *debut* event before any access is granted to the object. This *debut* event should be specified in the event list when the DM application sets its event disposition. The *debut* event gives the DM application the ability to download information (such as event lists and managed region information) that may be needed by the DMAPI implementation. Most likely, when downloading a new event list for an object, the list will not include the *debut* event, but only include events that require some action to be performed by the DM application.

The *debut* event is the first indication given to a DM application that a primitive DMAPI implementation is going to perform an operation on a file. The DM application can take this opportunity to download all the necessary information for that particular file, or for other files as well. Alternately, some DM applications may want to intercept the *mount* event to prime primitive DMAPI implementations, rather than having to receive many *debut* events.

The following functions for managing event lists on a file system objects are provided:

- *dm_set_eventlist*( )
  Specify the events, with the exception of the managed region events, to be generated for an object.
- *dm_get_eventlist*( )
  Get the list of events to be generated for an object.

2.11.4 Receiving and Responding to Events

Pending events can be received one at a time or in bulk. For synchronous events, a response to each event message is required. For all events, the only valid response is an indication of whether the operation should be continued or aborted. If the operation is to be aborted, an error can also be specified that will be returned to the user process in the form of an *errno*.

Event messages are variable length. This is because two of the primary fields of most event messages, file handles and path names, are variable length. DM applications should use *dm_get_config*( ) to determine the largest message size to size their buffers for calls to *dm_get_events*( ). For more information on accessing and manipulating variable length message buffers, see Data Structures definitions in Chapter 4.

The process that generated the event is blocked until the response is received by the DMAPI implementation. The sleep may or may not be interruptible; the implementation of the DMAPI will need to define the behavior for each synchronous event.

When a synchronous event message is generated, a token is part of the message. The token identifies the event message, and may reference access rights that are conveyed as part of the event message. No tokens are passed in an asynchronous messages.

When a DM application responds to a data event message, the token may reference access rights. If a DM application allows the operation to continue with the DM_RESP_CONTINUE return code, then special care must be taken by the implementation of the DMAPI to allow the operation that caused the event generation to continue without another DM application changing the state of the file.

Consider the following example:

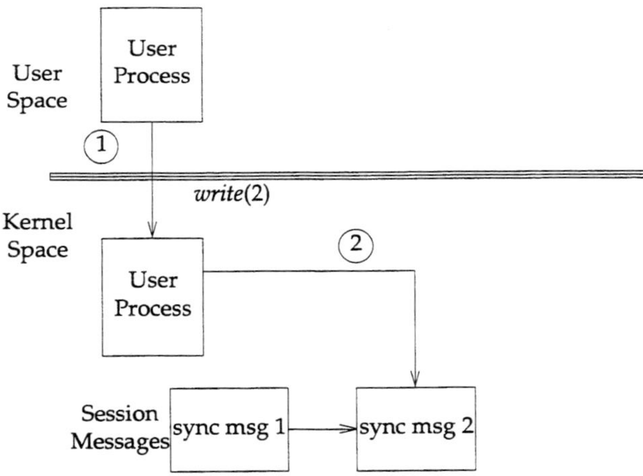

Figure 2-7 Event Generation with No Rights

In Figure 2-7. the user process has initiated a *write*(2) operation in user space, shown as step 1. When the application begins executing the Operating System code that performs the operation in the kernel, it detects that it must generate a synchronous managed region *write* event. The event message is enqueued on the session in step 2, and the user process is then awaited.

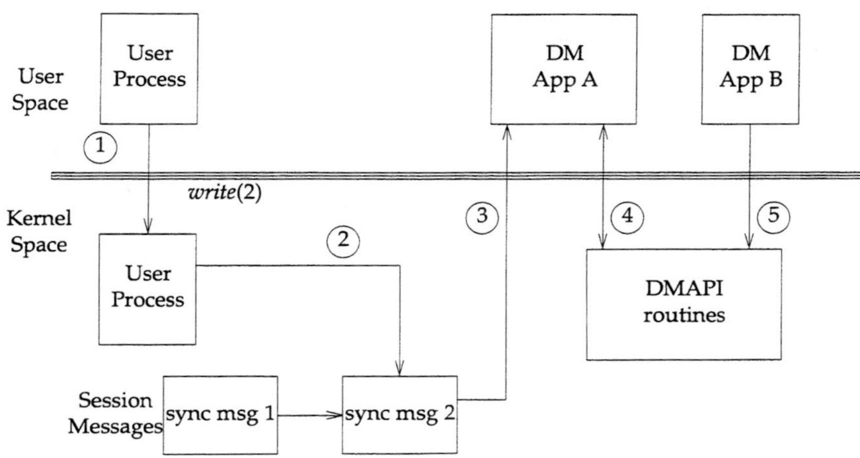

Figure 2-8 Requesting Access Rights after Event Generation

In Figure 2-8, the event message has been enqueued on the session in step 2, and is delivered to DM application A via *dm_get_events*( ) in step 3. Since the event message conveys no rights, DM application A must obtain access rights to the object. In this example, it requires the DM_RIGHT_EXCL right, which it obtains in step 4. At the same time, DM application B attempts to get exclusive access to the file in step 5. Since the access right is not available, DM application B will wait.

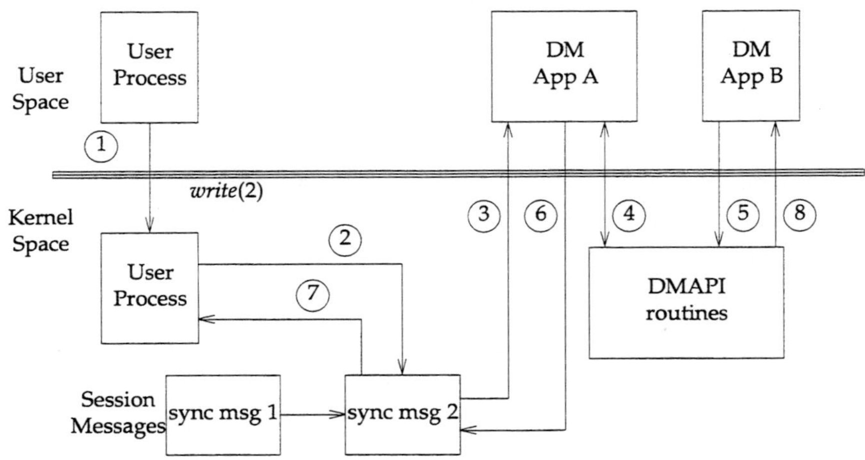

Figure 2-9 Continuing an Event with Access Rights

In Figure 2-9, DM application A has completed its processing in step 6 and continues the operation via a *dm_respond_event*( ) with the DM_RESP_CONTINUE response code. At the point when the function returns to the DM application (not explicitly shown, but it can be assumed to be a step 6a), the token that referenced the access rights to the object is invalid. However, the DMAPI implementation cannot immediately release the rights referenced by the token and grant them to someone else.

In step 7, the user process that caused the data event to be generated is resumed by the Operating System, and continues operation at the point at which the event was generated. Once the DMAPI implementation has completed whatever event processing it deems necessary, and once it has acquired whatever locks it needs to complete the rest of the *write*(2) operation, the access rights can be released. At this point, DM application B can be allowed to obtain the DM_RIGHT_EXCL access right, in step 8.

Rationale:

DM applications are logical extensions of the file system. When a DM application has completed the servicing of an event, it should appear as though the conditions that caused the event to be generated no longer exist. From the standpoint of the Operating System, it is as though the event never occurred; whatever state that required the event to be generated has been taken care of by the DM application.

In the example above, if DM application B were allowed to gain exclusive access to the file, it could possibly change the state of the file; all the recently-completed work of DM application A would then be void. More importantly, the implementation of the DMAPI would have no way to tell what state the file is in, unless it monitored all the actions of DM application B. It is also important to prevent the user process from starvation. Therefore, the user process should be allowed to continue its processing after DM application A has completed the event servicing.

The following functions for receiving event messages and responding to synchronous messages are provided:

- *dm_get_events*( )
  Get the next available event or events.
- *dm_respond_event*( )
  Respond to a synchronous event.

Some DM applications may be multi-threaded (or made up of multiple processes). To facilitate the processing of events between related processes, the DMAPI provides a method to move an outstanding event message from one session to another. The event message remains in the outstanding state, even though it is now enqueued on a different session.

The following function is provided:

- *dm_move_event*( )
  Move an event from one session to another.

If a DM application knows that it will take some significant period of time to process an event, the application can optionally notify the DMAPI implementation. The implementation is free to use or ignore the information.

The following function is provided:

- *dm_pending*( )
  Notify the file system of a slow DM application operation.

When a destroy event occurs, a DM application may optionally receive one DM attribute value in the event message by specifying to the DMAPI implementation which DM attribute name it wants to receive at destroy time.

The following function is provided:

- *dm_set_return_on_destroy*( )
  Specify a DM attribute to return with destroy events.

2.11.5 Pseudo Events

Pseudo events do not correspond to an event generated as a result of an operation in the operating system, such as a *write*(2). They are created by the DM application for purposes of generating a token or sending a message to a session. The actual message data is opaque to the DMAPI implementation. For the format of the pseudo-event, see Pseudo Events Section 3.6 on page 38. There is currently only one type of pseudo event; the *user* event.

As described in the Tokens Section 2.4 on page 10, tokens are always associated with a synchronous event message. To gain access to an object, a DM application must first create a message that contains the context for a token. The required access right can then be obtained via *dm_request_right*( ). *dm_create_userevent*( ) will create a synchronous event message of type **user** and enqueue it on the indicated session. The message and its corresponding token are outstanding. From the standpoint of the DMAPI, the message appears to have been delivered to a DM application via *dm_get_events*( ), but has not yet been responded to via *dm_respond_event*( ). The message will continue to exist until the DM application does a *dm_respond_event*( ) with the token.

For purposes of recovery processing, intelligent DM applications can use the user-generated event message mechanism to log their state during long and complicated operations. For example, if a DM application requires exclusive access to a file, it first needs to create a synchronous message. It puts together a user-level event message describing the operation, and then requests that a token be generated and associated with this pseudo-event message. If the DM application aborts (via a bus error, kill signal, etc.) before responding to the event, when it restarts, it can obtain the message and any corresponding state. This can provide the application with valuable information about its state when it aborted.

User-created messages can also be used as a test mechanism, to ensure that communications between the DMAPI implementation and a DM application are working correctly. Applications can use *dm_send_msg*( ) to create a synchronous or asynchronous message and have it enqueued on any specified session. The created message is also of type user, and contains the data specified by the user. For synchronous messages, the function does not return until the message has been responded to. Obviously, the process initiating the message via *dm_send_msg*( ) must not also be responsible for consuming the message via *dm_get_events*( ), or it will hang.

The following functions for creating a user level event message exist:

- *dm_create_userevent*( )
  Generate a user pseudo-event message and return its token. The message is placed on the session's outstanding event message queue.

- *dm_send_msg*( )
  Generate a user pseudo-event message and send it to the indicated session. The message is placed on the session's undelivered message queue.

2.12 Configuration Information

In order for a DM application to determine information about the underlying implementation of the DMAPI, an interface exists to interrogate various implementation specific details. The function *dm_get_config*( ) is called on a per-file system basis. Based on selected options in this function, it will return information as listed in its man-page definition (see *dm_get_config*( ) on page 89).

2.13 Limited Backup and Restore Support

Many current vendor migration and backup applications require additional interfaces into the DMAPI in order to fully support their functionality. To ease a vendor's transition to the DMAPI, a set of optional DM interfaces may be provided. They consist of the following functions:

- *dm_create_by_handle*( )
  Create a file system object using a DM handle.
- *dm_mkdir_by_handle*( )
  Create a directory object using a DM handle.
- *dm_symlink_by_handle*( )
  Create a symbolic link using a DM handle.

Chapter 3

Event Types

3.1 Overview

This chapter enumerates the types of events that can be generated, explains the data sent with the event message, and indicates what rights if any will be conveyed to the receiver of the event message.

Each event message consists of a common portion and an event specific portion. The common portion consists of the event type, a token, a sequence number, and the length of the data.

The common portion will not be shown in the following descriptions of events. For specific information on the layout of event messages, see Event Message Types, Section 4.7 on page 47.

There are five classes of events:

- file system administration
- namespace
- data
- metadata
- pseudo events.

Events can be either synchronous or asynchronous, as determined by the event type. Synchronous events allow a DM application to take action before an operation is continued by the operating system. For all events, it is not possible for a DM application to implement the operation in user space as though it were part of the operating system.

The DM application can respond to synchronous events in a number of ways. The operation can be continued, or it can be aborted with a specified error code returned back to the originating user process. For the *mount* event, the DM application can instruct the DMAPI implementation that it is not interested in the event, and the event should be sent to another session — see Setting Event Disposition, Section 2.11.1 on page 19 for more information. Some DMAPI implementations may also support a *retry* response to a *nospace* event. If *retry* is supported, the operation will be retried by the operating system if the response to *nospace* is DM_RESP_CONTINUE. Support of a retry is indicated by the DM_CONFIG_WILL_RETRY boolean returned via *dm_get_config*( ).

Asynchronous messages inform the DM application of the success or failure of an operation in the Operating System. They are delivered asynchronously with respect to the process performing the operation and offer no opportunity for a DM application to affect the requesting process; thus they are for notification purposes rather than for control.

Due to their asynchronous nature, there is no inherent upper bound on the number of undelivered asynchronous messages that may be queued on a session. Therefore implementations must choose either a reliable or an unreliable model for asynchronous messages.

In the reliable model, no asynchronous messages are ever lost. However, this requires that once the number of undelivered asynchronous messages reaches an implementation-defined maximum, processes attempting to generate additional messages are blocked until previously queued messages are delivered.

In the unreliable model, the implementation may simply drop messages when the undelivered message count exceeds an implementation limit.

A conforming DMAPI implementation shall document which model it provides for asynchronous messages. It is recommended that implementations adopt a reliable model, or failing that, an unreliable model that provides reliable semantics in all but the most unusual cases.

For synchronous messages, tokens identify the message. Each synchronous event message may convey the access rights that are required by the DM application; however, it is not guaranteed. The same message may even convey different access rights, depending on the code path taken in the operating system. DM applications must use the *dm_query_right*( ) and *dm_request_right*( ) interfaces to obtain the proper access rights for their operations. For asynchronous messages, there is no token.

3.1.1 Implementation Responsibilities

The DMAPI implementation must specify for each event the behavior, in the case that an event needs to be generated but no session has been established to receive the event message. This is different from the case where a session exists but there is no process to receive the event message (for example, the DM application has died). Some implementation alternatives are discussed in Undeliverable Events, Section 6.11 on page 172.

The implementation of the DMAPI will also need to define whether each individual synchronous event is interruptible. Since placement of events in the operating system is not defined by the DMAPI, interruptibility cannot be mandated by this interface specification.

3.1.2 Interruptible Events

If an implementation provides interruptible events, it must guarantee that event messages which convey access rights cannot vanish out from underneath a DM application while a DM operation is in progress.

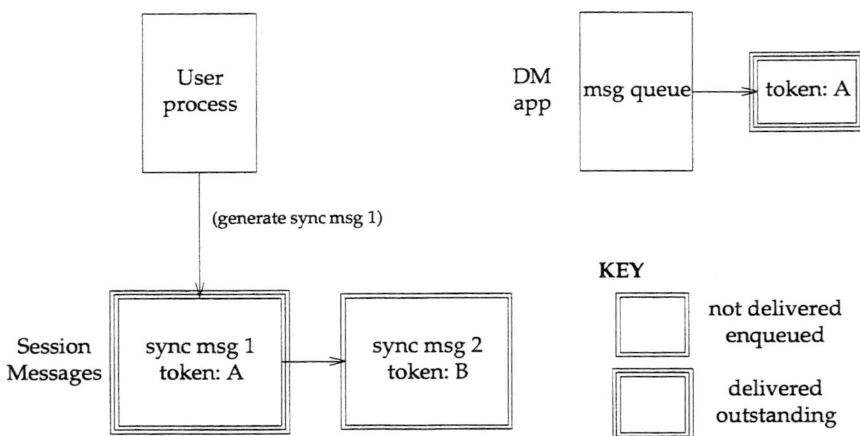

Figure 3-1 Interrupting a Synchronous Message

In Figure 3-1, the user has performed an operation that caused a synchronous event message, sync msg1, to be generated. The message has been received by the DM application, and is being processed. Assume the message conveyed rights to the DM application. If the implementation allows the user to interrupt the operation that caused the event message, the DMAPI implementation must complete any DM operation that is in progress for the associated event token, before processing the user interruption signal and returning control to the user thread. The DMAPI implementation must also clean up any outstanding access rights associated with the token, if the token is about to become invalid.

It is important to note that a DM application that is restartable depends on the existence of event messages to determine the state of the application before it died. Therefore, the DMAPI implementation must always keep the session message queues in an orderly state. If a token is invalidated by a user interruption, all state associated with that token must be cleaned up by the DMAPI implementation.

3.1.3 Asynchronous Namespace Event Delivery

Asynchronous namespace event messages are always generated for operations that succeed. It is implementation defined as to whether or not an asynchronous event message is sent for a failed operation.

3.1.4 Invalid Handles

Namespace event messages and *mount* event can contain invalid handles. For example, a DMAPI implementation may deliver an invalid handle for an object which belongs to a file system type that is not supported by this implementation of DMAPI. Call the *dm_handle_is_invalid* ( ) function to determine if the handle is valid.

3.2 File System Administration Events

3.2.1 mount

This event is generated at the point of a mount operation where the operation will succeed, but access to the file system has not yet been granted. This event allows DM applications to initialize, and provides them with the filesystem handle. This event is synchronous.

The *mount* event is unlike other events in that it may be sent to multiple sessions; see Section 2.11.2 on page 21 for more information. Any DMAPI interface that interacts only with the objects referenced by the handles supplied in the *mount* event, using the token supplied in the *mount* event, will work while the *mount* event token is held. All other DMAPI calls are undefined during *mount*.

The event message contains the following specific information:

fs handle	filesystem handle.
mountpoint handle	handle for the directory to be mounted over, maybe invalid.
mountpoint path	path name of the directory to be mounted over.
media designator	file system media designator.
mode	0 or DM_MOUNT_RDONLY.
root handle	handle for the root inode of the mounted file system.

3.2.2 preunmount

This event is generated at the point of an *unmount* operation where the operation is about to check for open files. Events for this file system may still be generated after the *preunmount* event. This allows the DM application to close any active accesses and ''cd'' out of the file system so that a DM application itself does not cause an *unmount* to fail. This event is synchronous.

The event message contains the following specific information:

fs handle	filesystem handle.
rootdir handle	handle to the root directory of the file system.
unmount mode	0 or DM_UNMOUNT_FORCE.

3.2.3 unmount

This event is generated after the operating system has attempted to *unmount* a file system. A return code of zero indicates the *unmount* was successful, and the file system is no longer mounted. Once unmounted, the DMAPI will not generate any other events for the file system until it is remounted. A non-zero return code indicates the *unmount* attempt failed. The reason for failure is given by the value of the return code. The DMAPI will continue to generate events for the file system after a failed *unmount*. The DMAPI implementation will always continue the operation, ignoring the response code from the DM application. This event is synchronous.

The event message contains the following specific information:

fs handle	filesystem handle.
unmount mode	0 or DM_UNMOUNT_FORCE.
retcode	return code of the operation (0 or errno).

3.2.4 nospace

This event is generated when an operation fails with ENOSPC. If the DMAPI implementation supports operation retry (DM_CONFIG_WILL_RETRY in the *dm_get_config*( ) function), a DM_RESP_CONTINUE response will cause the operation that produced the ENOSPC error to be generated to be retried. This event is synchronous.

The event message contains the following specific information:

fs handle	filesystem handle for file system where the ENOSPC error occurred.

3.2.5 debut

If the *debut* event is specified when a DM application registers via *dm_set_disp*( ), the DMAPI implementation will generate this event at least once before any of the set of other possible events are generated for the object. The *debut* event provides a mechanism for managing non-persistent attributes. It gives the DM application an opportunity to reset managed regions and event lists each time an object becomes active. If the DMAPI implementation supports persistent managed regions and persistent event lists (DM_CONFIG_PERS_MANAGED_REGIONS and DM_CONFIG_PERS_EVENTS in the *dm_get_config*( ) function), this event may not be generated. For DMAPI implementations that do not provide persistent storage of managed regions or event lists, the DM application should set the managed region list and a specific event list for the object. Most likely, the event list will not include the *debut* event, but instead will only include events that require some action to be performed by the DM application.

DMAPI implementations that do not support persistent non-opaque DM attributes directly are not required to support *debut* events; they may implement the functionality of the *debut* event through other internal mechanisms. This event is synchronous and optional.

The event message contains the following specific information:

object handle	object that is being accessed.

3.3 Namespace Events

Namespace operations allow a DM application to permit or deny an operation from continuing in the operating system. The synchronous events are generated before the operation has completed; there is no guarantee that the operation will be successful, however. Asynchronous namespace event messages are always generated for operations that succeed. It is implementation defined as to whether or not an asynchronous event message is sent for a failed event.

The DMAPI guarantees the ordering of paired namespace events. Asynchronous *post* event messages will always be generated after synchronous *before* event messages. If there are multiple synchronous events on a directory entry, it is not guaranteed that the associated asynchronous events are properly interleaved.

Namespace event messages are generated based on the directory entry that is being affected. If a DM application wants to receive namespace events for every file in the file system, it should do a *dm_set_eventlist*( ) using the filesystem handle.

3.3.1 create

This event is generated before the operating system adds a new entry to a directory. This event is synchronous. There is no guarantee that the operation will be successful.

The event message contains the following specific information:

parent handle	parent directory where entry name will be added.
entry name	name of the new entry.
mode	type of the object to be created and is the same value as *st_mode* in struct **stat** and *dt_mode* in struct **dm_stat**.

The DM application can either allow the operation to continue (DM_RESP_CONTINUE) or return an error code.

3.3.2 postcreate

This event is generated after the operating system has attempted to add an entry to a directory. This event is asynchronous.

The event message contains the following specific information:

parent handle	parent directory where entry name was added.
entry handle	handle for the new entry.
entry name	entry name that was added to the directory.
mode	type of the object created and is the same value as *st_mode* in struct **stat** and *dt_mode* in struct **dm_stat**.

retcode return code of the operation (0 or *errno*).

3.3.3 remove

This event is generated before the operating system removes an entry from a directory. This event is synchronous. There is no guarantee that the operation will be successful.

The event message contains the following specific information:

parent handle parent directory where entry name will be removed.

entry name entry name to be removed from the directory.

mode type of the object to be removed and is the same value as *st_mode* in struct **stat** and *dt_mode* in struct **dm_stat**.

The DM application can either allow the operation to continue (DM_RESP_CONTINUE) or return an error code.

3.3.4 postremove

This event is generated after the operating system has attempted to remove an entry from a directory. This event is asynchronous.

The event message contains the following specific information:

parent handle parent directory where entry name was removed.

entry name entry name removed from the directory.

mode type of the object removed and is the same value as *st_mode* in struct **stat** and *dt_mode* in struct **dm_stat**.

retcode return code of the operation (0 or *errno*).

3.3.5 rename

This event is generated before the operating system renames a directory entry in a file system. This event is synchronous. There is no guarantee that the operation will be successful.

The event message contains the following specific information:

old parent handle original parent directory where old entry name resides.

new parent handle new parent directory where new entry name is to be added.

old entry name directory entry to be renamed.

new entry name new name of directory entry.

The DM application can either allow the operation to continue (DM_RESP_CONTINUE) or return an error code.

3.3.6 postrename

This event is generated after the operating system has attempted to rename an entry in a file system. This event is asynchronous.

The event message contains the following specific information:

old parent handle	original parent directory where old entry name resided.
new parent handle	new parent directory where new entry name was added.
old entry name	original directory entry that was renamed.
new entry name	new name of directory entry.
retcode	return code of the operation (0 or *errno*).

3.3.7 symlink

This event is generated before the operating system adds a new symbolic link entry in a directory. This event is synchronous. There is no guarantee that the operation will be successful.

The event message contains the following specific information:

parent handle	parent directory where symlink entry name will be added.
symlink entry name	name of symbolic link entry.
symlink contents	contents of symbolic link.

The DM application can either allow the operation to continue (DM_RESP_CONTINUE) or return an error code.

3.3.8 postsymlink

This event is generated after the operating system has attempted to add a symbolic link entry in a directory. This event is asynchronous.

The event message contains the following specific information:

parent handle	parent directory where symlink entry name was added.
entry handle	handle for the new symlink entry.
symlink entry name	entry name of newly added symbolic link.
symlink contents	contents of symbolic link.
retcode	return code of the operation (0 or *errno*).

3.3.9 link

This event is generated before the operating system adds a new hard link entry in a directory. This event is synchronous. There is no guarantee that the operation will be successful.

The event message contains the following specific information:

parent handle	parent directory where target entry name will be added.
source link handle	handle of entry to be linked to.
target entry name	new link name to be added to the directory.

The DM application can either allow the operation to continue (DM_RESP_CONTINUE) or return an error code.

3.3.10 postlink

This event is generated after the operating system has attempted to add a new hard link entry in a directory. This event is asynchronous.

The event message contains the following specific information:

parent handle	parent directory where target entry name was added.
source link handle	handle of entry that was linked to.
target entry name	new link name added to the directory.
retcode	return code of the operation (0 or *errno*).

3.4 Data Events

Data events are triggered by interactions with managed regions. They are synchronous, and allow the DM application to take some action before the operation is continued in the operating system. Data events only occur on regular files.

3.4.1 read

This event is generated when a *read* of a file overlaps one or more managed regions that have the event set in the managed region *flags* field. This event is synchronous. The event message contains the following specific information:

file handle	handle for file being read.
offset	starting offset of *read* operation.
length	length in bytes of *read* request.

3.4.2 write

This event is generated when a *write* to a file overlaps one or more managed regions that have the event set in the managed region *flags* field. This event is synchronous.

The event message contains the following specific information:

file handle	handle for file being written.
offset	starting offset for *write* operation.
length	length in bytes of *write* request.

3.4.3 truncate

This event is generated when the operating system attempts a truncation of a file that overlaps one or more managed regions that has the event set in the managed region *flags* field. This event can be generated directly in response to a truncate request by the user, as from *truncate*(2), or indirectly as when an existing file is truncated via *open*(2) with the appropriate flags. This event is synchronous.

The event message contains the following specific information:

file handle	handle for file being truncated.
offset	starting offset for truncation operation.

3.5 Metadata Events

3.5.1 attribute

This event is generated when an object is changed in a way that affects the change time (*dt_ctime*) value returned by *dm_get_bulkattr*( ), dm_get_dirattrs or *dm_get_fileattr*( ). This event is asynchronous.

The event message contains the following specific information:

object handle	object that was affected.

3.5.2 cancel

This event may be generated when the implementation determines that an earlier request is no longer of interest (for example, if a user terminated an application program). The method of determining that a request is no longer of interest is implementation-dependent. The DM application may react to this event according to its preference; however, the original event, the one being cancelled, must still receive a response such as DM_RESP_ABORT or DM_RESP_CONTINUE. This event is asynchronous.

The intent of this event message is that in advising a DM application that a given result is no longer of interest, the DM application might be better able to schedule resources that might otherwise have been devoted to providing that given result. This scheduling may be particularly advisable if long-latency resources were required to satisfy a request.

The data associated with the cancel event is in the **dm_cancel_event_t** format. The event message contains the following specific information:

sequence	the value of the ev_sequence field for the event being canceled.
token	the token of the original event.

This event is optional.

3.5.3 close

This event is generated on the close of a file system object. (The definition of "close" is implementation-dependent. Typically, it will be on the last close.) This notification is a hint only, and is not guaranteed to be reliable. This event is asynchronous and optional.

The event message contains the following specific information:

object handle	object that is being closed.

3.5.4 destroy

This event is generated when the Operating System has destroyed an object. If the destroyed object had the attribute specified by *dm_set_return_on_destroy*( ), a copy of its attribute data will be returned with the event message. The attribute data may be truncated if it was longer than the maximum supported length for the implementation (returned by *dm_get_config*( ) with the DM_CONFIG_MAX_ATTR_ON_DESTROY flag). This event is asynchronous.

The destroy event message contains the following specific information:

object handle	object that was destroyed.
attribute name	attribute name being returned.

attribute copy	copy of attribute data for the object.

3.6 Pseudo Events

Pseudo events are events that do not correspond to any operation in the Operating System. Currently, the only defined pseudo event is the user event that is generated by both *dm_create_userevent*( ) and *dm_send_msg*( ).

3.6.1 user event format

This event structure is used in the *dm_create_userevent*( ) and *dm_send_msg*( ) functions for both synchronous and asynchronous events. All *dm_create_userevent*( ) functions create synchronous event messages. The *dm_send_msg*( ) function can be either synchronous or asynchronous. Only synchronous events will associate a token with the event message. Asynchronous events can be indicated by a value of DM_INVALID_TOKEN in the token field. DM applications can use this event type to store information that is associated with the message that is to be created. The message data is not interpreted by the DMAPI implementation.

For more information see the Tokens Section 2.4 on page 10 and the Events Section 2.11 on page 19.

Since this is not a generated event, the entire event message will be shown, and is as follows:

event type	set to DM_EVENT_USER.
token	token that will be returned or DM_INVALID_TOKEN.
message length	length of the data to follow.
data	private data that the DM application wants to have associated with a message.

3.7 Event Summary

A summary of events, the type of objects they are delivered on, and how they are enabled, is given in Table 3-1.

Event	Sync/Async	Enabled By	Enabled On
mount	sync	always enabled	global
preunmount	sync	*dm_set_eventlist*	fs
unmount	sync	*dm_set_eventlist*	fs
nospace	sync	*dm_set_eventlist*	fs
debut	sync	*always enabled*	file, dir or fs
create	sync	*dm_set_eventlist*	dir or fs
postcreate	async	*dm_set_eventlist*	dir or fs
remove	sync	*dm_set_eventlist*	dir or fs
postremove	async	*dm_set_eventlist*	dir or fs
rename	sync	*dm_set_eventlist*	dir or fs
postrename	async	*dm_set_eventlist*	dir or fs
symlink	sync	*dm_set_eventlist*	dir or fs
postsymlink	async	*dm_set_eventlist*	dir or fs
link	sync	*dm_set_eventlist*	dir or fs
postlink	async	*dm_set_eventlist*	dir or fs
read	sync	*dm_set_region*	managed region
write	sync	*dm_set_region*	managed region
truncate	sync	*dm_set_region*	managed region
attribute	async	*dm_set_eventlist*	file, dir or fs
cancel	async	*dm_set_eventlist*	file, dir or fs
close	async	*dm_set_eventlist*	file, dir or fs
destroy	async	*dm_set_eventlist*	file, dir or fs
user	either	*created by dm_create_userevent and dm_send_msg*	not applicable

Table 3-1 Event Summary

Table 3-2 lists the objects that the DMAPI implementation will consult to determine if an event should be generated. For example, the *rename* event will be generated if a *rename*( ) occurs where one of the following objects has that event enabled:

- old parent directory
- new parent directory
- filesystem handle for the file system containing the object to be renamed.

Event	Controlling Object Handle
mount	global
preunmount	fs
unmount	fs
nospace	fs
debut	file, dir or fs
create	parent dir or fs
postcreate	parent dir or fs
remove	parent dir or fs
postremove	parent dir or fs
rename	old parent, new parent, or fs
postrename	old parent, new parent, or fs
symlink	parent dir or fs
postsymlink	parent dir or fs
link	parent dir or fs
postlink	parent dir or fs
read	file
write	file
truncate	file
attribute	file, dir or fs
cancel	file, dir or fs
close	file, dir or fs
destroy	file, dir or fs
user	n/a

Table 3-2 Event Generation Objects

Events are defined via a number of different data structures. Table 3-3 summarizes the event structures that are used to deliver each event.

Event	Data structure
mount	**dm_mount_event**
preunmount	**dm_namesp_event**
unmount	**dm_namesp_event**
nospace	**dm_namesp_event**
debut	**dm_namesp_event**
create	**dm_namesp_event**
postcreate	**dm_namesp_event**
remove	**dm_namesp_event**
postremove	**dm_namesp_event**
rename	**dm_namesp_event**
postrename	**dm_namesp_event**
symlink	**dm_namesp_event**
postsymlink	**dm_namesp_event**
link	**dm_namesp_event**
postlink	**dm_namesp_event**
read	**dm_data_event**
write	**dm_data_event**
truncate	**dm_data_event**
attribute	**dm_namesp_event**
cancel	**dm_cancel_event**
close	**dm_namesp_event**
destroy	**dm_destroy_event**
user	**opaque to DMAPI implementation**

Table 3-3 Event Data Structures

A number of different events use the **dm_namesp_event** structure. Table 3-4 lists which fields are valid, and their contents, for each event message that uses this structure.

Event	handle1	handle2	name1	name2	mode	retcode
preunmount	fs	rootdir	-	-	unmount mode	-
unmount	fs	-	-	-	unmount mode	r/c
nospace	fs	-	-	-	-	-
debut	object	-	-	-	-	-
create	parent	-	name	-	st_mode	-
postcreate	parent	new	name	-	st_mode	r/c
remove	parent	-	name	-	st_mode	-
postremove	parent	-	name	-	st_mode	r/c
rename	old parent	new parent	old name	new name	-	-
postrename	old parent	new parent	old name	new name	-	r/c
symlink	parent	-	name	contents	-	-
postsymlink	parent	new	name	contents	-	r/c
link	parent	source	name	-	-	-
postlink	parent	source	name	-	-	r/c
attribute	object	-	-	-	-	-
close	object	-	-	-	-	-

-	not applicable
r/c	return code

Table 3-4 Field Use in the dm_namesp_event Structure

The following table describes the fields of the *dm_mount_event*.

mode	mount options
handle1	file system handle
handle2	mounted-on directory handle, may be invalid
name1	mount path
name2	file system media
roothandle	root inode handle

Table 3-5 Field Use in the dm_mount_event Structure

Chapter 4

Data Structures

The DMAPI references a number of data structures that are presented here in alphabetical order. All of these structures can have additional vendor-specific fields unless otherwise stated. Many of the interfaces deal with variable length data, such as handles and path names. This data is encapsulated in the implementation defined **dm_vardata_t** structure, see the Implementation Notes section for one proposed definition. To access the data, the following functions are provided:

```
DM_GET_VALUE(p, field, type)
```

```
DM_GET_LEN(p, field)
```

Rationale:

The philosophy behind all the interfaces that deal with variable length data is to allow for such data to be embedded in the same buffer as the structure that contains a reference to it. The references are all relative to the start of the structure containing them, so that buffers containing such structures can be copied without destroying the embedded references. The expectation is that the variable length data will most commonly be appended directly after the structure that references it, but the **dm_vardata_t** interface does not demand this spatial relationship. However, the interfaces that return variable length data are designed (and implicitly specified) so that this spatial relationship does hold for the information they return.

To access fields within a variable length structure, the DM application must use the macros defined above. For example, to get at the handle in an event message, the following code could be used:

```
dm_eventmsg_t        *msg = malloc(bufsize);
dm_data_event_t      *event;

dm_get_events(sid, ....msg,...);
event = DM_GET_VALUE(msg, data, dm_data_event_t *);
hanp  = DM_GET_VALUE(event, handle, void *);
hlen  = DM_GET_LEN(event, handle);
```

A number of DMAPI functions return lists of variable length structures. To move from one structure to the next in a list, the following macro should be used:

```
#define DM_STEP_TO_NEXT(struct_ptr, struct_type)
```

A suggested implementation of the DM_STEP_TO_NEXT macro is given under Section 6.10 on page 172.

The following table shows the affected structures:

Structure Name
dm_attrlist_t
dm_dispinfo_t
dm_eventmsg_t
dm_stat_t

Table 4-1 Structures used in Lists

The DM_STEP_TO_NEXT macro can be used as shown in the following example:

```
dm_stat_t     *statbuf = malloc(bufsize);
dm_stat_t     *sbufp;

dm_init_attrloc(...)
dm_get_bulkattr(sid, ...statbuf);

sbufp = statbuf;
while (sbufp != NULL) {
    ......
    sbufp = DM_STEP_TO_NEXT(sbufp, dm_stat_t *);
}
```

4.1 dm_attrlist_t

SYNOPSIS

```
struct dm_attrlist {
    dm_attrname_t     al_name;
    dm_vardata_t      al_data;
};
typedef struct dm_attrlist     dm_attrlist_t;
```

DESCRIPTION

A *dm_attrlist_t* pointer is passed to *dm_getall_dmattr*( ) to retrieve all persistent data management attributes associated with the specified file. The data structure includes, but is not limited to, the fields described above.

Since attributes may have different size data fields, use the DM_GET_VALUE and DM_GET_LEN macros to interpret the al_data field. All attribute names are fixed length 8 byte (defined as DM_ATTR_NAME_SIZE) opaque values.

Each attribute may store up to DM_CONFIG_MAX_ATTRIBUTE_SIZE bytes of data per file. The value of DM_CONFIG_MAX_ATTRIBUTE_SIZE is obtained via *dm_get_config*( ) and has a lower bound of 32 bytes. The total amount of space available for storage of all persistent attributes on a file system is bounded by DM_CONFIG_TOTAL_ATTRIBUTE_SPACE.

4.2 dm_attrloc_t

DESCRIPTION

An opaque scalar that is used in the *dm_get_bulkattr*( ) and *dm_init_attrloc*( ) functions.

4.3 dm_attrname_t

SYNOPSIS

```
struct dm_attrname {
    u_char an_chars[DM_ATTR_NAME_SIZE];
};
typedef struct dm_attrname    dm_attrname_t;
```

DESCRIPTION

This is used by the data management attribute functions to identify an attribute. All attribute names are fixed length 8 byte (defined as DM_ATTR_NAME_SIZE) opaque values.

It is recommended that applications use printable eight character names (or pad smaller names with the NULL character) to simplify display of attributes names and use a predefined three byte prefix as specified in section 3.10.2.

4.4 dm_boolean_t

DESCRIPTION

An opaque scalar that can contain either DM_TRUE or DM_FALSE.

4.5 dm_config_t

REQUIREMENT

This enumeration must contain at least the elements listed here. The DMAPI implementation may choose a different order for the elements.

SYNOPSIS

```
typedef enum {
    DM_CONFIG_INVALID,
    DM_CONFIG_BULKALL,
    DM_CONFIG_CREATE_BY_HANDLE,
    DM_CONFIG_DTIME_OVERLOAD,
    DM_CONFIG_LEGACY,
    DM_CONFIG_LOCK_UPGRADE,
    DM_CONFIG_MAX_ATTR_ON_DESTROY,
    DM_CONFIG_MAX_ATTRIBUTE_SIZE,
    DM_CONFIG_MAX_HANDLE_SIZE,
    DM_CONFIG_MAX_MANAGED_REGIONS,
    DM_CONFIG_MAX_MESSAGE_DATA,
    DM_CONFIG_OBJ_REF,
    DM_CONFIG_PENDING,
    DM_CONFIG_PERS_ATTRIBUTES,
    DM_CONFIG_PERS_EVENTS,
    DM_CONFIG_PERS_INHERIT_ATTRIBS,
    DM_CONFIG_PERS_MANAGED_REGIONS,
    DM_CONFIG_PUNCH_HOLE,
    DM_CONFIG_TOTAL_ATTRIBUTE_SPACE,
    DM_CONFIG_WILL_RETRY
} dm_config_t;
```

DESCRIPTION

Enums from **dm_config_t** are used in *dm_get_config*() calls to query various options pertaining to the implementation of the DMAPI.

4.6 dm_dispinfo_t

SYNOPSIS

```
struct dm_dispinfo {
    dm_vardata_t     di_fshandle;
    dm_eventset_t    di_eventset;
};
typedef struct dm_dispinfo    dm_dispinfo_t;
```

DESCRIPTION

The **dm_dispinfo_t** structure is used on calls to *dm_getall_disp*() to retrieve the list of all event dispositions for all file systems for a given session. DM applications should use the DM_GET_VALUE macro to retrieve the value of the filesystem handle and DM_STEP_TO_NEXT to move between successive structures.

4.7 Event Message Types

4.7.1 dm_eventmsg_t

SYNOPSIS

```
struct dm_eventmsg {
    dm_eventtype_t      ev_type;
    dm_token_t          ev_token;
    dm_sequence_t       ev_sequence;
    dm_vardata_t        ev_data;
};
typedef struct dm_eventmsg     dm_eventmsg_t;
```

DESCRIPTION

Every event message is of type **dm_eventmsg_t**. Since multiple messages can be returned in a single call, DM applications must use the DM_STEP_TO_NEXT macro to move from one message to the next.

All event messages contain an event type. Synchronous messages also contain a token. The **dm_eventmsg_t** structure represents this common data via the *ev_type* and *ev_token* fields. Asynchronous messages never have a token associated with them; therefore *ev_token* will always be DM_INVALID_TOKEN for asynchronous messages.

The rest of the contents of the message for a given event is distinct for an event's type, and will be contained in a *dm_xxx_event* buffer, where *xxx* depends on the event type. As with other data whose size or type isnt known in advance, it is referred to through the DM_GET_VALUE macro applied to a descriptor field that lives in the common prelude part of the event message.

ev_type
The event type that occurred.

ev_token
The token may reference and identify a specific access right for a handle in the event-specific portion of the message. When responding to the message, the token is used to identify the message and is no longer valid when the response call *dm_respond_event*( ) has completed. The token field is valid for synchronous messages only; the field will be DM_INVALID_TOKEN for asynchronous event messages.

ev_sequence
This is a sequence identifier for the event message. If the implementation supports the *cancel* event, the value of this sequence identifier must be unique in the event stream. A subsequent *cancel* event may refer to this event using the value of this sequence identifier. The contents of this field is not specified if the *cancel* event is not supported.

ev_data
The event-specific data.

4.7.2 dm_cancel_event_t

SYNOPSIS

```
struct dm_cancel_event {
     dm_sequence_t    ce_sequence;
     dm_token_t       ce_token;
};
typedef struct dm_cancel_event    dm_cancel_event_t;
```

DESCRIPTION

The **dm_cancel_event** structure is used for the *cancel* event message type.

4.7.3 dm_data_event_t

SYNOPSIS

```
struct dm_data_event {
     dm_vardata_t    de_handle;
     dm_off_t        de_offset;
     dm_size_t       de_length;
};
typedef struct dm_data_event    dm_data_event_t;
```

DESCRIPTION

The **dm_data_event** structure is used for all *data* events.

4.7.4 dm_destroy_event_t

SYNOPSIS

```
struct dm_destroy_event {
     dm_vardata_t     ds_handle;
     dm_attrname_t    ds_attrname;
     dm_vardata_t     ds_attrcopy;
};
typedef struct dm_destroy_event    dm_destroy_event_t;
```

DESCRIPTION

The **dm_destroy_event** structure is used for the *destroy* event.

4.7.5 dm_mount_event_t

SYNOPSIS

```
struct dm_mount_event {
     mode_t          me_mode;
     dm_vardata_t    me_handle1;
     dm_vardata_t    me_handle2;
     dm_vardata_t    me_name1;
     dm_vardata_t    me_name2;
     dm_vardata_t    me_roothandle;
};
typedef struct dm_mount_event     dm_mount_event_t;
```

DESCRIPTION

The **dm_mount_event** structure is used for the *mount* event.

4.7.6 dm_namesp_event_t

SYNOPSIS

```
struct dm_namesp_event {
    mode_t          ne_mode;
    dm_vardata_t    ne_handle1;
    dm_vardata_t    ne_handle2;
    dm_vardata_t    ne_name1;
    dm_vardata_t    ne_name2;
    int             ne_retcode;
};
typedef struct dm_namesp_event    dm_namesp_event_t;
```

DESCRIPTION

The **dm_namesp_event** structure is used for all *namespace* events.

4.8 dm_eventset_t

DESCRIPTION

To specify events, the **dm_eventset_t** type must be used. This is an opaque type (to the DM application) that is manipulated via the DMEV_ZERO, DMEV_SET and DMEV_CLR macros in a manner analogous to the FD_SET type that is used in calls to *select*(2).

4.9 dm_eventtype_t

REQUIREMENT

This enumeration must contain at least the elements listed here. The DMAPI implementation may choose a different order for the elements.

SYNOPSIS

```
typedef enum {
    DM_EVENT_INVALID,
    DM_EVENT_CLOSE,
    DM_EVENT_MOUNT,
    DM_EVENT_PREUNMOUNT,    DM_EVENT_UNMOUNT,
    DM_EVENT_NOSPACE,
    DM_EVENT_DEBUT,
    DM_EVENT_CREATE,        DM_EVENT_POSTCREATE,
    DM_EVENT_REMOVE,        DM_EVENT_POSTREMOVE,
    DM_EVENT_RENAME,        DM_EVENT_POSTRENAME,
    DM_EVENT_SYMLINK,       DM_EVENT_POSTSYMLINK,
    DM_EVENT_LINK,          DM_EVENT_POSTLINK,
    DM_EVENT_READ,
    DM_EVENT_WRITE,
    DM_EVENT_TRUNCATE,
    DM_EVENT_ATTRIBUTE,
    DM_EVENT_CANCEL,
    DM_EVENT_DESTROY,
    DM_EVENT_USER,
    DM_EVENT_MAX
} dm_eventtype_t;
```

DESCRIPTION

Event types are encoded in message structures and **dm_eventset_t** types as *dm_eventtype_t* enums. DM_EVENT_MAX is guaranteed to be larger than the number of the largest valid event type that can be represented in the **dm_eventset_t** type. DM_EVENT_INVALID is guaranteed to be smaller than the number of the smallest valid event type that can be represented in the *dm_eventset_t* type.

4.10 dm_extent_t

SYNOPSIS

```
struct dm_extent {
        dm_extenttype_t       ex_type;
        dm_off_t              ex_offset;
        dm_size_t             ex_length;
};
typedef struct dm_extent    dm_extent_t;
```

DESCRIPTION

The extent structures returned by the call to *dm_get_allocinfo*( ) contains the *ex_type* field, whose value is one of two indicators for the type of extent. If a DMAPI implementation can know that an extent of a file would be read as zeros, for example because no media resources are mapped to that extent of the file, it should indicate that knowledge about the extent by associating DM_EXTENT_HOLE with that extent. Otherwise, the value DM_EXTENT_RES should be associated with that extent. The *ex_offset* field is the byte offset into the file where the extent begins, and *ex_length* is the byte count of the extent.

4.11 dm_extenttype_t

SYNOPSIS

```
typedef enum {
        DM_EXTENT_INVALID,
        DM_EXTENT_RES,
        DM_EXTENT_HOLE
} dm_extenttype_t;
```

DESCRIPTION

The **dm_extenttype_t** enum is used to specify the type of extent in the **dm_extent_t** structure.

4.12 dm_fileattr_t

SYNOPSIS

```
struct dm_fileattr {
    mode_t      fa_mode;
    uid_t       fa_uid;
    gid_t       fa_gid;
    time_t      fa_atime;
    time_t      fa_mtime;
    time_t      fa_ctime;
    time_t      fa_dtime;
    dm_off_t    fa_size;
} ;
typedef struct dm_fileattr dm_fileattr_t;
```

DESCRIPTION

These are the fields that can be modified by *dm_set_fileattr*( ).

4.13 DM Handles

SYNOPSIS

```
void        *hanp;
size_t       hlen;
```

DESCRIPTION

Handles are opaque to DM applications. The length of a handle is implementation defined. When a handle must be used in a function, it is specified using two parameters. The hlen parameter specifies the length of the opaque data that is pointed to by hanp.

When a handle is embedded in a structure, the **dm_vardata_t** structure is used. The DM application should use the DM_GET_VALUE macro to access the handle data and DM_GET_LEN to determine the length of the opaque handle data.

4.14 dm_fsid_t

DESCRIPTION

This is a scalar used to represent a file system identifier.

4.15 dm_igen_t

DESCRIPTION

This is a scalar used to represent a file inode generation number.

4.16 dm_inherit_t

SYNOPSIS

```
struct dm_inherit {
    dm_attrname_t    ih_name ;
    mode_t           ih_filetype;
};
typedef struct dm_inherit    dm_inherit_t;
```

DESCRIPTION

A *dm_inherit_t* pointer is passed to *dm_getall_inherit*( ) to retrieve all data management attributes that have been made inheritable through the *dm_set_inherit*( ) function. The call is made on a per file system basis. The ih_filetype field is the type of the file as defined in Single UNIX Specification.

4.17 dm_msgtype_t

SYNOPSIS

```
typedef enum {
    DM_MSGTYPE_INVALID,
    DM_MSGTYPE_SYNC,
    DM_MSGTYPE_ASYNC
} dm_msgtype_t;
```

DESCRIPTION

This is used when creating a user event via *dm_send_msg*( ) to specify the type of event message that should be created, synchronous or asynchronous.

4.18 dm_off_t

DESCRIPTION

This is a signed scalar used to represent file offsets.

> **Rationale:**
> Vendors have taken different approaches for extending file addressibility beyond the off_t type, which is usually 32 bits. For example, some vendors have an offset_t type or an off64_t type for working with files larger than 2GB.

The intent is that **dm_off_t** be a suitable type for addressing all files supported by the system.

4.19 dm_region_t

SYNOPSIS

```
struct dm_region {
    dm_off_t     rg_offset;
    dm_size_t    rg_size;
    u_int        rg_flags;
};
typedef struct dm_region    dm_region_t;
```

DESCRIPTION

The **dm_region** structure defines the range of bytes that are managed in the file. The rg_flags field can be set to generate synchronous *read*, *write*, and *truncate* events whenever the associated operation is performed within the managed region. A region may extend outside the current valid portions of a file. If rg_size is set to zero, then that region extends from rg_offset through EOF and beyond. Thus operations beyond the end of file, including appends and sparse writes, will generate events according to the flag setting. This means that the *rg_flags* field must always be set to a valid state. Regions may also be allocated with no associated events set by using DM_REGION_NOEVENT. This may be used to allocate space for future control of a region of the file in DMAPI implementations that provide persistent managed regions.

Valid values for the rg_flags field are as follows:

DM_REGION_READ
: Generate synchronous event for *read* operations that overlap this managed region

DM_REGION_WRITE
: Generate synchronous event for *write* operations that overlap this managed region

DM_REGION_TRUNCATE
: Generate synchronous event for *truncate* operations that overlap this managed region

DM_REGION_NOEVENT
: Do not generate any events for this managed region.

4.20 Region Flags

DEFINES

```
#define DM_REGION_NOEVENT      xxx
#define DM_REGION_READ         xxx
#define DM_REGION_WRITE        xxx
#define DM_REGION_TRUNCATE     xxx
```

DESCRIPTION

The defines above are used to specify the generation of events in the *rg_flags* field of the managed region structure. DM_REGION_READ, DM_REGION_WRITE and DM_REGION_TRUNCATE may be ORed together.

4.21 dm_response_t

REQUIREMENT

This enumeration must contain at least the elements listed here. The DMAPI implementation may choose a different order for the elements.

SYNOPSIS

```
typedef enum {
    DM_RESP_INVALID,
    DM_RESP_CONTINUE,
    DM_RESP_ABORT,
    DM_RESP_DONTCARE
} dm_response_t;
```

DESCRIPTION

When a DM application responds to an event via *dm_respond_event*(), the response codes must be an enum taken from **dm_response_t**.

4.22 dm_right_t

SYNOPSIS

```
typedef enum {
    DM_RIGHT_NULL,
    DM_RIGHT_SHARED,
    DM_RIGHT_EXCL
} dm_right_t;
```

DESCRIPTION

The **dm_right_t** enum specifies the access rights for an object.

4.23 dm_sequence_t

DESCRIPTION:

This is an unsigned scalar used to represent one of a sequence of event messages for message cancellation.

4.24 dm_sessid_t

DESCRIPTION:

The session ID is an opaque scalar. Implementations of the DMAPI may differ in the information they require to be stored with the session ID. A special value, DM_NO_SESSION, is available for use as an invalid or non-existent session.

4.25 dm_size_t

DESCRIPTION

This is an unsigned scalar used to represent sizes of extents within files (among other things).

4.26 dm_ssize_t

DESCRIPTION

This is a signed scalar used for function calls that return the size of the file or -1 to indicate error.

4.27 dm_stat_t

SYNOPSIS

```
struct dm_stat {
    dm_vardata_t      dt_handle;
    dm_vardata_t      dt_compname;
    dm_eventset_t     dt_emask;
    int               dt_nevents;
    int               dt_pers;
    int               dt_pmanreg;
    time_t            dt_dtime;
    u_int             dt_change;

    dev_t             dt_dev;
    ino_t             dt_ino;
    mode_t            dt_mode;
    nlink_t           dt_nlink;
    uid_t             dt_uid;
    gid_t             dt_gid;
    dev_t             dt_rdev;
    dm_off_t          dt_size;
    time_t            dt_atime;
    time_t            dt_mtime;
    time_t            dt_ctime;
    u_int             dt_blksize;
    dm_size_t         dt_blocks;
};
typedef struct dm_stat    dm_stat_t;
```

DESCRIPTION

The **dm_stat** structure is used for retrieving per file attributes via the *dm_get_fileattr*( ), *dm_get_dirattrs*( ) and *dm_get_bulkattr*( ) functions. The structure is composed of at least fields found in the Single UNIX Specification **struct stat** as well as additional DMAPI specific fields.

Since handles are variable length, the structure is somewhat problematic as *dm_get_bulkattr*( ) can return a variable number of variable length structures. To access the variable length data in an individual structure, the DM_GET_VALUE macro should be used. To move between structures, the DM_STEP_TO_NEXT macro is used.

The **dm_stat** structure contains at least the following fields:

dt_handle
A **dm_vardata_t** structure that contains the offset from the beginning of the structure where the data for the handle begins. The DM_GET_VALUE macro should be used to access the handle.

dt_compname
A **dm_vardata_t** structure that contains the offset from the beginning of the structure where the name of the file begins. This field is valid only for *dm_get_dirattrs*( ). The DM_GET_VALUE macro should be used to access the file name.

dt_emask
The event bindings that are stored persistently with the file. The event types in this set can be manipulated by the *dm_set_eventlist*( ) functions.

Not all DMAPI implementations support persistent event bindings. Support can be determined through use of the *dm_get_config*( ) function.

dt_nevents
The number of events in the event mask, dt_emask.

dt_pers
A boolean indicating whether the file does or does not have associated persistent opaque data management attributes. A non-zero value indicates presence of persistent attributes.

dt_pmanreg
A boolean indicating whether the file does or does not have associated persistent managed regions. A non-zero value indicates presence of persistent managed regions.

dt_dtime
The value of the data management attribute time stamp if dt_pers is a non-zero value. This field may be the same as ctime as determined by calling *dm_get_config*( ) with DM_CONFIG_DTIME_OVERLOADED.

This field will be set to zero if persistent attributes are not supported by the DMAPI or associated with this file.

dt_change
This field is a file change indicator that is changed on each file modification (of either data or metadata) and on each persistent attribute change. It can be used by DM applications during lock upgrade to determine whether the file has changed state. If the same value is returned in dt_change between two calls, the file is guaranteed not to have changed; however, some implementations of the DMAPI may return a different dt_change value even if the file has not really been modified.

The following fields are taken from the Single UNIX Specification **struct stat**.

dt_dev
ID of device containing file

dt_ino
File serial number

dt_mode
Mode of file

dt_nlink
Number of links to the file

dt_uid
User ID of file

dt_gid
Group ID of file

dt_rdev
Device ID (if file is character/block special)

dt_size
File size in bytes (if file is regular file)

dt_atime
Time of last access

dt_mtime
Time of last data modification

dt_ctime
Time of last status change

dt_blksize
A file system specific preferred I/O block size for this object. In some file system types, this may vary from file to file.

dt_blocks
Number of blocks of a file system-specific size allocated for this object.

4.28 dm_timestruct_t

SYNOPSIS

```
struct dm_timestruct {
    time_t   dm_tv_sec;
    int32    dm_tv_nsec;
};
typedef struct dm_timestruct dm_timestruct_t;
```

DESCRIPTION

A **dm_timestruct_t** is the structure passed to *dm_pending*( ), used to represent an interval of time in seconds and nanoseconds. It contains at least the following information:

dm_tv_sec

dm_tv_nsec

4.29 dm_token_t

DESCRIPTION

A **dm_token_t** is an opaque scalar. There are two distinguished values, DM_NO_TOKEN, which signifies automatic token acquisition, and DM_INVALID_TOKEN, which signifies no legal value.

4.30 dm_vardata_t

DESCRIPTION

A **dm_vardata_t** is an opaque structure. Implementations of the DMAPI may differ in the information they require to be stored in a variable length data structure. Use the macros as mentioned at the beginning of this chapter to access **dm_vardata_t** fields. See the Implementation Notes chapter for an example definition of the **dm_vardata_t** structure and its access macros.

4.31 dm_xstat_t

SYNOPSIS

```
struct dm_xstat {
    dm_stat_t       dx_statinfo;
    dm_vardata_t    dx_attrdata;
};
typedef struct dm_xstat    dm_xstat_t;
```

DESCRIPTION

The **dm_xstat** structure is used for retrieving per file attributes and one persistent data management attribute via *dm_get_bulkall*( ). The data structure includes, but is not limited to, the fields described above.

The **dm_xstat** structure contains at least the following fields:

dx_statinfo The **dm_stat_t** structure

dx_attrdata The attribute data for the object as set by *dm_set_dmattr*( ) on the object.

4.32 Attribute Mask Defines

DEFINES

```
#define DM_AT_ATIME         xxx
#define DM_AT_CFLAG         xxx
#define DM_AT_CTIME         xxx
#define DM_AT_DTIME         xxx
#define DM_AT_EMASK         xxx
#define DM_AT_GID           xxx
#define DM_AT_HANDLE        xxx
#define DM_AT_MODE          xxx
#define DM_AT_MTIME         xxx
#define DM_AT_PATTR         xxx
#define DM_AT_PMANR         xxx
#define DM_AT_SIZE          xxx
#define DM_AT_STAT          xxx
```

```
#define DM_AT_UID            xxx
```

DESCRIPTION

The #defines shown above are used by the *dm_get_bulkall*( ), *dm_get_bulkattr*( ), *dm_get_dirattrs*( ), *dm_get_fileattr*( ) and *dm_set_fileattr*( ) functions. They are OR-able flags. For descriptions of these flags, see the man-page definitions for these functions. in Chapter 5 on page 63.

4.33 Get Events Defines

DEFINES

```
#define DM_EV_WAIT           xxx
```

DESCRIPTION

There is currently one definition used for retrieving DM messages via *dm_get_events*( ). This definition is an OR-able flag. Refer to the *dm_get_events*( ) reference manual page for a description of this flag.

4.34 Mount Event Defines

DEFINES

```
#define DM_MOUNT_RDONLY           xxx
```

DESCRIPTION

The possible flags contained in the me_mode field of the **dm_mount_event** structure during the *mount* event. These definitions are OR-ed flags. The DM_MOUNT_RDONLY flag is set when the mount command is run with the read-only option set.

4.35 Request Right Defines

DEFINES

```
#define DM_RR_WAIT           xxx
```

DESCRIPTION

There is currently one definition used for requesting rights via *dm_request_right*( ). This definition is an OR-able flag. Refer to the *dm_request_right*( ) reference manual page for a description of this flag.

4.36 Unmount Event Defines

DEFINES

```
#define DM_UNMOUNT_FORCE      xxx
```

DESCRIPTION

The possible flags contained in the ne_mode field of the **dm_namesp_event** structure during the *preunmount* and *unmount* events. These definitions are OR-ed flags. The DM_UNMOUNT_FORCE flag is set when the *unmount* command is run with the *force unmount* option set.

4.37 Invisible Write Defines

DEFINES

```
#define DM_WRITE_SYNC           xxx
```

DESCRIPTION

There is currently one flag definition for the flags parameter to *dm_write_invis*( ). This definition is an OR-able flag. Refer to the *dm_write_invis*( ) reference manual page for a description of this flag.

4.38 Miscellaneous Defines

DEFINES

```
#define DM_SESSION_INFO_LEN     xxx
#define DM_NO_SESSION           xxx

#define DM_TRUE                 xxx
#define DM_FALSE                xxx

#define DM_INVALID_TOKEN        xxx
#define DM_NO_TOKEN             xxx

#define DM_INVALID_HANP         xxx
#define DM_INVALID_HLEN         xxx

#define DM_GLOBAL_HANP          xxx
#define DM_GLOBAL_HLEN          xxx

#define DM_VER_STR_CONTENTS     xxx

#define DM_ATTR_NAME_SIZE       8
```

DESCRIPTION

The #defines shown above are referenced by various DMAPI functions. The DMAPI does not mandate their value, as is indicated by the xxx. Each implementation of the DMAPI is free to chose a suitable value.

DM_SESSION_INFO_LEN is the length of the string that can be associated with the session on the *dm_create_session*( ) call. 256 bytes is the recommended length.

DM_NO_SESSION is used on *dm_create_session*( ) to indicate that session assumption is not wanted. The implementation of the DMAPI should choose a meaningful value.

DM_TRUE and DM_FALSE are boolean values used in several functions such as *dm_get_bulkattr*( ) and *dm_get_fileattr*( ).

DM_INVALID_TOKEN is a special token value which signifies no legal token value.

DM_NO_TOKEN is a special token value which is used in calls to functions that require a token but the caller wants the DM implementation to automatically acquire the appropriate rights.

DM_INVALID_HANP and DM_INVALID_HLEN are used to specify invalid handles.

DM_GLOBAL_HANP and DM_GLOBAL_HLEN are used to specify the global handle.

DM_VER_STR_CONTENTS specifies the DMAPI implementation specific version string as returned from the *dm_init_service*( ) function.

DM_ATTR_NAME_SIZE specifies the fixed length of an attribute name in bytes.

Chapter 5

DMAPI Definitions

The following pages describe the interfaces of the DMAPI in detail. The interfaces are given in man-page format, and are in alphabetical order. In the man-pages, parameters are described as follows:

(I) indicates an input parameter

(O) indicates an output parameter

(I/O) indicates both an input and an output parameter.

Many of the following functions reference data structures that are defined by the DMAPI. To provide a consistent API from platform to platform, these data structures are defined in a header file named **<dmapi.h>**. DM applications that need to use these functions must include this header file. The specification of this header file is not shown on the following function definitions, but is of the following format:

```
#include <dmapi.h>
```

There are two paradigms used for DMAPI functions:

- *iterative*
  which allow DM applications to make repeated calls to the same function to obtain all available data
- *non-iterative*
  which require a DM application to provide a buffer large enough to hold all available data in a single call.

The error conditions specified in these man-pages are the recommended values. A DMAPI implementation may recognize and report additional error conditions.

A number of the functions are optional in the DMAPI specification. It is left to an implementation as to whether those optional functions are supported. If an optional function is not supported, it must still be implemented as a stub function that returns -1 and sets errno to ENOSYS. A DM application can use the *dm_get_config*() function to also determine which optional functions are supported by an implementation rather than having to first call the function and check for ENOSYS.

5.1 Non-iterative Functions

Several functions accept and return variable length data structures, such as *dm_get_dmattr*( ). Other functions may return a variable number of structures in a list, such as *dm_getall_inherit*( ). Both these function types use the E2BIG paradigm. In this paradigm, the DM application specifies the size of the buffer in one of the input arguments. If the buffer is not large enough to hold the requested information, then no data is copied, the error E2BIG is returned, and one of the output arguments is updated to indicate the required size of the buffer.

There are two distinct flavors of the E2BIG paradigm:

- functions which return variable sized data structures
- functions which return a variable number of fixed size structures.

Generally, functions that return variable sized structures specify the size of the input buffer in bytes via the buflen parameter. If E2BIG is returned, then the parameter *rlenp* is set to the required buffer size. These types of functions take a *void* * pointer to a buffer.

Functions that return fixed size structures specify the number of elements that fit in the input buffer, via the *nelem* parameter. If [E2BIG] is returned, the *nelemp* parameter is updated to indicate the number of elements that are available. DM applications can use this return value to resize their buffer. These types of functions take a buffer pointer to a specific type.

This is summarized in the following table:

Parameters	**Function type**	**Buffer Type**
buflen / rlenp	variable length structures	*void* *
nelem / nelemp	variable number of structures	specific structure pointer

Table 5-1 Non-iterating Function Types

5.2 Iterating Functions

Several DMAPI functions are iterating functions, allowing the DM application to make a number of calls to the same function to retrieve all the available data. These functions typically contain an offset parameter, providing the DM application with the ability to specify the starting point in a file or file system for data retrieval.

These functions return -1 on error and set the global *errno* to indicate the cause of error. If a zero is returned, the function completed successfully, and no more data is available. If the function completed successfully, but more data maybe available, a value of 1 is returned.

The following functions are the only iterating functions:

Function Name
dm_get_allocinfo( )
dm_get_bulkall( )
dm_get_bulkattr( )
dm_get_dirattrs( )

Table 5-2 Iterating Functions

5.3 DMAPI Macros

The following reference manual page defines the 4 DMAPI macros:

DMEV_CLR	remove an event from an event list
DMEV_ISSET	determine if an event is set in an event list
DMEV_SET	add an event to an event list
DMEV_ZERO	initialize the event list to contain no events

NAME

DMEV_CLR — remove an event from an event list
DMEV_ISSET — determine if an event is set in an event list
DMEV_SET — add an event to an event list
DMEV_ZERO — initialize the event list to contain no events

SYNOPSIS

```
int
DMEV_SET(
    dm_eventtype_t      event_type,
    dm_eventset         event_list)

int
DMEV_CLR(
    dm_eventtype_t      event_type,
    dm_eventset         event_list)

int
DMEV_ISSET(
    dm_eventtype_t      event_type,
    dm_eventset         event_list)

void
DMEV_ZERO(
    dm_eventset         event_list)
```

DESCRIPTION

These macros manipulate event sets as defined by *dm_eventset_t*. DMEV_SET() adds the specified *event_type* to the *event_list* set, while DMEV_CLR() removes the specified event from the list. DMEV_ISSET() evaluates to non-zero if the specified *event_type* is a member of the *event_list* set, otherwise it evaluates to zero. DMEV_ZERO() initializes the *event_list* set to contain no events.

SEE ALSO

dm_get_eventlist(), *dm_set_eventlist*().

5.4 DMAPI Functions

The following reference manual pages define the DMAPI function calls. These functions are all listed in column 1 of Table 5-3.

In some cases, a single reference manual page definition covers several functions. These cases are identified in column 2 of Table 5-3. In these cases, the man-page title is stylized to reflect the functions it covers. In addition, where space for this title on the man-page does not allow the function names to be concatenated, a descriptive name reflecting the nature of the common operation is enclosed in braces ''{ }''.

Table 5-3 DMAPI Functions

Function	Reference Manual Page Title
dm_clear_inherit( )	
dm_getall_inherit( )	
dm_set_inherit( )	
dm_create_by_handle( )	
dm_mkdir_by_handle( )	
dm_symlink_by_handle( )	
dm_sync_by_handle( )	
dm_create_session( )	
dm_destroy_session( )	
dm_getall_sessions( )	
dm_query_session( )	
dm_set_return_on_destroy( )	
dm_downgrade_right( )	
dm_query_right( )	
dm_release_right( )	
dm_request_right( )	
dm_upgrade_right( )	
dm_get_allocinfo( )	
dm_get_bulkall( )	**dm_get_{bulkattributes}( )**
dm_get_bulkattr( )	**dm_get_{bulkattributes}( )**
dm_get_dirattrs( )	**dm_get_{bulkattributes}( )**
dm_get_config( )	
dm_get_dmattr( )	
dm_getall_dmattr( )	
dm_remove_dmattr( )	
dm_set_dmattr( )	

Function	Reference Manual Page Title
dm_create_userevent( )	
dm_find_eventmsg( )	
dm_get_events( )	
dm_get_eventlist( )	
dm_get_config_events( )	
dm_move_event( )	
dm_respond_event( )	
dm_set_eventlist( )	
dm_get_fileattr( )	
dm_set_fileattr( )	
dm_get_mountinfo( )	
dm_get_region( )	
dm_set_region( )	
dm_getall_disp( )	
dm_getall_tokens( )	
dm_handle_cmp( )	
dm_handle_is_valid( )	
dm_handle_hash( )	
dm_handle_to_fshandle( )	
dm_handle_to_path( )	
dm_make_handle( )	**dm_handle_{construct/extract}( )**
dm_make_fshandle( )	**dm_handle_{construct/extract}( )**
dm_handle_to_fsid( )	**dm_handle_{construct/extract}( )**
dm_handle_to_igen( )	**dm_handle_{construct/extract}( )**
dm_handle_to_ino( )	**dm_handle_{construct/extract}( )**
dm_fd_to_handle( )	**dm_fd/path_to_handle & dm_handle_free()**
dm_path_to_fshandle( )	**dm_fd/path_to_handle & dm_handle_free()**
dm_path_to_handle( )	**dm_fd/path_to_handle & dm_handle_free()**
dm_handle_free( )	**dm_fd/path_to_handle & dm_handle_free()**
dm_init_attrloc( )	
dm_init_service( )	
dm_obj_ref_hold( )	**dm_obj_ref_hold/release/query( )**
dm_obj_ref_rele( )	**dm_obj_ref_hold/release/query( )**
dm_obj_ref_query( )	**dm_obj_ref_hold/release/query( )**

Function	Reference Manual Page Title
dm_pending( )	
dm_punch_hole( )	**dm_punch/probe_hole( )**
dm_probe_hole( )	**dm_punch/probe_hole( )**
dm_read_invis( )	**dm_read/write_invis( )**
dm_write_invis( )	**dm_read/write_invis( )**
dm_send_msg( )	
dm_set_disp( )	

NAME

dm_clear_inherit — clear an attribute's inherit-on-create status

SYNOPSIS

```
int
dm_clear_inherit(
    dm_sessid_t     sid,
    void           *hanp,
    size_t          hlen,
    dm_token_t      token,
    dm_attrname_t  *attrnamep)
```

DESCRIPTION

The *dm_clear_inherit*( ) function marks the named attribute as no longer inheritable on the specified file system.

dm_sessid_t *sid* (I)
The identifier for the session of interest.

void **hanp* (I)
The filesystem handle.

size_t *hlen* (I)
The length of the handle in bytes.

dm_token_t *token* (I)
The token referencing the access right for the file system handle. The access right must be DM_RIGHT_EXCL or the token DM_NO_TOKEN may be used and the interface acquires the appropriate rights.

dm_attrname_t **attrnamep* (I)
The attribute name that marks the name as no longer inheritable.

RETURN VALUE

Zero is returned on success. On error, -1 is returned, and the global *errno* is set to one of the following values:

[EACCES]
The access right referenced by the token for the handle is not DM_RIGHT_EXCL.

[EBADF]
The filesystem handle does not refer to an existing or accessible object.

[EFAULT]
The system detected an invalid address in attempting to use an argument.

[EINVAL]
The argument attrname specifies an attribute that has not been marked inheritable.

[EINVAL]
The argument token is not a valid token.

[EINVAL]
The session is not valid.

[EIO]
The attempt to clear the inheritable attribute resulted in an I/O error.

[ENOSYS]
The DMAPI implementation does not support this optional function.

[EPERM]
The caller does not hold the appropriate privilege.

SEE ALSO

dm_set_inherit( ), *dm_getall_inherit*( ).

NOTES

dm_clear_inherit( ) is an optional component of the DMAPI.

NAME

dm_create_by_handle — create a file system object using a DM handle

SYNOPSIS

```
int
dm_create_by_handle(
    dm_sessid_t    sid,
    void          *dirhanp,
    size_t         dirhlen,
    dm_token_t     token,
    void          *hanp,
    size_t         hlen,
    char          *cname)
```

DESCRIPTION

The *dm_create_by_handle*( ) function allows applications the ability to create an object in a directory specified by *dirhanp* and *with a component* name *cname* that can, after creation, be referenced by the supplied target handle *hanp*. This is useful when an application is reconstructing a file system object for which it still has the data and attributes stored on an alternate media.

It is the responsibility of the user of this function to reconstruct the object state including extended attributes. See *dm_set_fileattr*( ) and *dm_set_dmattr*( ).

If an object cannot be constructed by the file system for the specified handle, an error is returned.

dm_sessid_t *sid* (I)
: The identifier for the session of interest.

void **dirhanp* (I)
: The handle for the directory that contains the target file.

size_t *dirhlen* (I)
: The length of the directory handle in bytes.

dm_token_t *token* (I)
: The token referencing the access right for the directory handle. The access right must be DM_RIGHT_EXCL right or the token DM_NO_TOKEN may be used and the interface acquires the appropriate rights.

void **hanp* (I)
: The file handle of the object.

size_t *hlen* (I)
: The length of the file handle in bytes.

char **cname* (I)
: The name of the object to be created in the specified directory.

RETURN VALUE

Zero is returned on success. On error, -1 is returned, and the global *errno* is set to one of the following values:

[EACCES]
: The access right referenced by the token for the directory handle is not DM_RIGHT_EXCL.

[EBADF]
: The parent handle does not refer to an existing or accessible object.

[EEXIST]
The file handle refers to an existing object.

[EFAULT]
The system detected an invalid address in attempting to use an argument.

[EINVAL]
The argument token is not a valid token.

[EINVAL]
The session is not valid.

[ENOSYS]
The DMAPI implementation does not support this optional function.

[EPERM]
The caller does not hold the appropriate privilege.

SEE ALSO

dm_set_fileattr( ), *dm_set_dmattr*( ), *dm_mkdir_by_handle*( ), *dm_symlink_by_handle*( ).

NOTES

edm_create_by_handle( ) is an optional component of the DMAPI.

NAME

dm_create_session — create a session

SYNOPSIS

```
int
dm_create_session(
    dm_sessid_t    oldsid,
    char          *sessinfop,
    dm_sessid_t   *newsidp)
```

DESCRIPTION

The *dm_create_session*( ) function establishes a DMAPI session. Sessions are guaranteed to be unique as long as the system that grants them is up; sessions are not unique across reboots. Applications should treat the session id as opaque.

To later identify the session during recovery, an arbitrary string can be associated with the session. This NULL-terminated string must have a length of DM_SESSION_INFO_LEN bytes (including the NULL) or less. The *sessinfop* parameter is an arbitrary string; the DMAPI assigns no semantics to it whatsoever. It is not an error for more than one session to have identical *sessinfop* strings.

To support recovery, the DMAPI supports the notion of session assumption. This is provided by the *oldsid* parameter. If specified, the DMAPI atomically updates all messages that refer to *oldsid* to be associated with a new session id, which is returned to the caller. When *dm_create_session*( ) returns, *oldsid* is no longer valid; attempts to use it in subsequent DMAPI calls result in an error.

To determine a previous session identifier, the DM application can use *dm_getall_sessions*( ) and *dm_query_session*( ) to find a specific old session identifier. If *oldsid* is provided, then when *dm_create_session*( ) returns, the new session has assumed what was an active, open session. It is not necessary to register to receive events; the new session has assumed the context of the previous session, including all default event registrations. If a *sessinfop* string is provided, it replaces any existing *sessinfop* string associated with the old session.

Sessions are not tied to a particular process. Once a session has been established, any processes with sufficient permissions (such as the super-user) may use the session. This permits an application to hand a session off to another process for further operations. The hand off can be accomplished merely by conveying the value of the session ID to the other process via any mechanism (shared memory, message, pipe, file, etc.). Because sessions are not tied to any particular process, no DMAPI calls are needed to accomplish session hand off.

dm_sessid_t *oldsid* (I)
: A value previously returned by dm_create_session(), or DM_NO_SESSION if no assumption is desired.

char **sessinfop* (I)
: A NULL-terminated string of at most DM_SESSION_INFO_LEN to be associated with the session.

dm_sessid_t **newsidp* (O)
: The new session id created by the DMAPI.

RETURN VALUE

Zero is returned on success. On error, -1 is returned, and the global *errno* is set to one of the following values:

[E2BIG]
: sessinfop string was longer than DM_SESSION_INFO_LEN bytes.

[EFAULT]
The system detected an invalid address in attempting to use an argument.

[ENOMEM]
The DMAPI could not obtain the required resources to complete the call.

[EINVAL]
The argument oldsid contains an invalid session id.

[EPERM]
The caller does not hold the appropriate privilege.

SEE ALSO

dm_destroy_session( ), *dm_set_disp*( ), *dm_getall_sessions*( ), *dm_query_session*( ).

NAME

dm_create_userevent — generate a user pseudo-event message

SYNOPSIS

```
int
dm_create_userevent(
    dm_sessid_t    sid,
    size_t         msglen,
    void          *msgdatap,
    dm_token_t    *tokenp)
```

DESCRIPTION

Tokens are always associated with an event message. If a DM application needs to obtain a token to get specific access rights to an object, it must generate a pseudo-event message to define a context for that token.

DM applications can use the user defined message data to record information about the state of the operation they are performing. This information could be useful during recovery processing. The DMAPI implementation does not interpret the contents of the message data.

The *dm_create_userevent*( ) function allows a token to be associated with arbitrary message data. The DMAPI creates a new token, and associate it with an event message whose data is given by the *msgp* parameter. The message is enqueued on the specified session, and is in the same state as synchronous messages that have been received by DM applications via *dm_get_events*( ) but not yet responded to. The type of the message is set to be DM_EVENT_USER. The token is valid until the DM application does a *dm_respond_event*( ) on the token. The generated token does not reference any access rights for any object handles. DM applications must use *dm_request_right*( ) to obtain access rights.

dm_sessid_t *sid* (I)
The identifier for the session of interest.

size_t *msglen* (I)
The length of the message data in bytes.

void **msgdatap* (I)
The data that is to be included in the message.

dm_token_t **tokenp* (O)
A newly created token identifying the message.

RETURN VALUE

Zero is returned on success. On error, -1 is returned, and the global *errno* is set to one of the following values:

[E2BIG]
The user message data is too big to fit into implementation defined limits. The limit can be determined by calling the *dm_get_config*( ) function using the value DM_CONFIG_MAX_MESSAGE_DATA.

[EFAULT]
The system detected an invalid address in attempting to use an argument.

[EINVAL]
The session is not valid.

[ENOMEM]
The DMAPI could not obtain the required resources to complete the call.

[EPERM]
The caller does not hold the appropriate privilege.

SEE ALSO

dm_send_msg( ).

NAME

dm_destroy_session — destroy the specified session

SYNOPSIS

```
int
dm_destroy_session(
    dm_sessid_t    sid)
```

DESCRIPTION

To perform a graceful shutdown, DM applications must shut down and destroy a session as part of their termination procedures. Upon successful return from *dm_destroy_session*( ) the session id is invalid.

If the file system is active or the session is registered for any events, *dm_destroy_session*( ) cannot invalidate the session id. If there are any outstanding or undelivered events, *dm_destroy_session*( ) will fail.

dm_sessid_t *sid* (I)
: The session id to destroy.

RETURN VALUE

Zero is returned on success. On error, -1 is returned, and the global *errno* is set to one of the following values:

[EBUSY]
: There are outstanding events for the session that have not been delivered, or there are synchronous events that have not been responded to.

[EINVAL]
: The session is not valid.

[EPERM]
: The caller does not hold the appropriate privilege.

SEE ALSO

dm_create_session()

NAME

dm_downgrade_right — downgrade an exclusive access right to a shared right

SYNOPSIS

```
int
dm_downgrade_right(
    dm_sessidt      sid,
    void           *hanp,
    size_t          hlen,
    dm_token_t      token)
```

DESCRIPTION

Downgrade an exclusive access right currently held for the object specified by the handle and referenced by the token. The downgrade operation does not drop the exclusive access right currently held for the object before acquiring the share right. The minimum right to hold when making this request is DM_RIGHT_EXCL.

dm_sessid_t *sid* (I)
: The identifier for the session of interest.

void **hanp* (I)
: The handle for the file system object for which downgrading access right is being requested and with which an exclusive access right is already associated.

size_t *hlen* (I)
: The length of the handle in bytes.

dm_token_t *token* (I)
: The token referencing the exclusive access right for the object to be manipulated

RETURN VALUE

Zero is returned on success. On error, -1 is returned, and the global *errno* is set to one of the following values:

[EBADF]
: The file handle does not refer to an existing or accessible object.

[EFAULT]
: The system detected an invalid address in attempting to use an argument.

[EINVAL]
: The token does not grant a DM_RIGHT_EXCL right to the specified object.

[ENOSYS]
: The DMAPI implementation does not support this optional function.

[ESRCH]
: The token does not refer to any outstanding DM event.

[EPERM]
: The caller does not hold the appropriate privilege.

[EPERM]
: The access right currently held is not DM_RIGHT_EXCL.

SEE ALSO

dm_release_right( ), *dm_request_right*( ), *dm_upgrade_right*( ).

NOTES

dm_downgrade_right( ) is an optional component of the DMAPI.

NAME

dm_find_eventmsg — get the message for the event

SYNOPSIS

```
int
dm_find_eventmsg(
    dm_sessid_t     sid,
    dm_token_t      token,
    size_t          buflen,
    void           *bufp,
    size_t         *rlenp)
```

DESCRIPTION

Obtains the message that is associated with the token. It is only possible to obtain messages that are outstanding, that is, messages that have been delivered but not responded to.

Tokens are always associated with an event message; receipt of a message is the only way a DM application can obtain a token. Once a message has been responded to, the token (and the corresponding message) is no longer valid.

dm_sessid_t *sid* (I)
: The identifier for the session of interest.

dm_token_t *token* (I)
: The token that corresponds to an outstanding event message.

size_t *buflen* (I)
: The length of the message buffer in bytes.

void **bufp* (O)
: The buffer that should be filled in with a dm_eventmsg structure.

size_t **rlenp* (O)
: The size of the requested information. If the buffer is not large enough to hold the requested information (as indicated by the *buflen* parameter), then no data is copied, the call fails with [E2BIG], and *rlenp* is set to the required size. *rlenp* is updated if either the call was successful or the call fails with [E2BIG], but is undefined otherwise.

RETURN VALUE

Zero is returned on success. On error, -1 is returned, and the global *errno* is set to one of the following values:

[E2BIG]
: The information is too large to fit into the buffer.

[EFAULT]
: The system detected an invalid address in attempting to use an argument.

[EINVAL]
: The session or token is not valid.

[ENOMEM]
: The DMAPI could not obtain the required resources to complete the call.

[EPERM]
: The caller does not hold the appropriate privilege.

SEE ALSO

dm_getall_tokens),( ) dm_getall_sessions( ), *dm_respond_event*( ), *dm_query_session*( ).

NAME

dm_get_allocinfo — return the current allocation information for a file

SYNOPSIS

```
int
Dm_get_allocinfo(
    dm_sessid_t     sid,
    void           *hanp,
    size_t          hlen,
    dm_token_t      token,
    dm_off_t       *offp,
    u_int           nelem,
    dm_extent_t    *extentp,
    u_int          *nelemp)
```

DESCRIPTION

The *dm_get_allocinfo*( ) function returns allocation information for a file. This function is iterative in nature and allows the application to begin retrieving extent information about a file at any byte offset.

The extent structures returned by the call to *dm_get_allocinfo*( ) contains the *ex_type* field, whose value is one of two indicators for the type of extent. If a DMAPI implementation can know that an extent of a file would be read as zeros, for example because no media resources are mapped to that extent of the file, it should indicate that knowledge about the extent by associating DM_EXTENT_HOLE with that extent. Otherwise, the value DM_EXTENT_RES should be associated with that extent. The *ex_offset* field is the byte offset into the file where the extent begins, and *ex_length* is the byte count of the extent.

dm_sessid_t *sid* (I)
: The identifier for the session of interest.

void **hanp* (I)
: The handle for the target file.

size_t *hlen* (I)
: The length of the handle in bytes.

dm_token_t *token* (I)
: The token referencing the access right for the handle. The access right must be at least DM_RIGHT_SHARED or the token DM_NO_TOKEN may be used and the interface acquires the appropriate rights.

dm_off_t **offp* (I/O)
: On output, the byte address of the beginning of the extent following the last returned extent. When **offp* returns zero, there are no more extents. On input, the byte address from which to start reporting extent information. Assigning zero to **offp* causes the initial extents of the file to be returned. Assigning the value returned by the previous call to *dm_get_allocinfo*( ) causes the next extents to be returned. The value in **offp* may point beyond the current size of the file.

u_int *nelem* (I)
: The number of elements in the extent array.

dm_extent_t **extentp* (O)
: The residency information for the file.

u_int **nelemp* (O)
: The number of elements returned.

RETURN VALUE

Zero indicates success and that no more information is available. 1 is returned on success and indicates more information maybe available. On error, -1 is returned and the global *errno* is set to indicate the error.

[EACCES]
The access right referenced by the token for the handle is not at least DM_RIGHT_SHARED.

[EBADF]
The file handle does not refer to an existing accessible object.

[EFAULT]
The system detected an invalid address in attempting to use an argument.

[EINVAL]
nelem is zero and must be at least one.

[EINVAL]
The argument offp does not point to a valid extent.

[EINVAL]
The file handle does not refer to a regular file.

[EINVAL]
The session is not valid.

[EINVAL]
The argument token is not a valid token.

[EIO]
An attempt to read the file residency information resulted in an I/O error.

[ENOTSUP]
This call is not meaningful for the object being checked.

[EPERM]
The caller does not hold the appropriate privilege.

SEE ALSO

dm_punch_hole( ), *dm_probe_hole*( ).

NAME

dm_get_bulkattr — get bulk attributes for an entire file system
dm_get_bulkall — get bulk data management attributes for a file system
dm_get_dirattrs — get bulk attributes for a directory

SYNOPSIS

```
int
dm_get_bulkattr(
    dm_sessid_t      sid,
    void            *hanp,
    size_t           hlen,
    dm_token_t       token,
    u_int            mask,
    dm_attrloc_t    *locp,
    size_t           buflen,
    void            *bufp,
    size_t          *rlenp)

int
dm_get_bulkall(
    dm_sessid_t      sid,
    void            *hanp,
    size_t           hlen,
    dm_token_t       token,
    u_int            mask,
    dm_attrname_t   *attrnamep,
    dm_attrloc_t    *locp,
    size_t           buflen,
    void            *bufp,
    size_t          *rlenp)

int
dm_get_dirattrs(
    dm_sessid_t      sid,
    void            *hanp,
    size_t           hlen,
    dm_token_t       token,
    u_int            mask,
    dm_attrloc_t    *locp,
    size_t           buflen,
    void            *bufp,
    size_t          *rlenp)
```

DESCRIPTION

The function *dm_get_bulkattr*() retrieves both standard file attributes and DM specific file attributes for the file system specified by the argument *hanp*. The *bufp* argument is filled with one or more **dm_stat** structures on return. The argument *mask* indicates which fields of the **dm_stat** structure to return (see Section 4.27 on page 55 for the flag definitions). For fields that are not returned, the corresponding fields of the **dm_stat** structure are undefined; the *dt_compname* field is always undefined. The file system specified by *hanp* must be mounted.

The function *dm_get_bulkall*() is similar to *dm_get_bulkattr*(), except that it returns a series of **dm_xstat** structures in the buffer identified by the *bufp* argument. The *dx_attrdata* field of each **dm_xstat** structure will contain the data associated with the attribute name that is specified by the *attrnamep* argument. If the named attribute is not set on a given file, that file will show a zero-length attribute in *dx_attrdata*. Because **dm_xstat** structures contain variable data, the output buffer should be traversed using the DM_STEP_TO_NEXT macro. *dm_get_bulkall*( ) is an optional interface in the DMAPI.

The *dm_get_dirattrs*( ) function performs a similar function for directories. It returns the file name, attributes, and DM specific file attributes for the files in the directory specified by *hanp*. The *bufp* argument is filled with one or more **dm_stat** structures on return. The argument *mask* indicates which fields of the **dm_stat** structure to return. For fields that are not returned, the corresponding fields of the **dm_stat** structure are undefined. The *dt_compname* field is always filled in. The directory specified by *hanp* must be on a mounted file system. If a file is named several times within the directory (that is, multiple links to the same file), a **dm_stat** structure is returned for each one.

These functions can be repeated, and each time fill the buffer *bufp* with zero or more **dm_stat** (or **dm_xstat**) structures, until all structures have been returned. The argument *locp* must be initialized via *dm_init_attrloc*( ) (see *dm_init_attrloc*( ) on page 117) before calling *dm_get_bulkattr*( ), *dm_get_bulkall*( ) or *dm_get_dirattrs*( ). The same handle must be used for initializing *locp* as is used for retrieving the attributes.

The arguments to *dm_get_bulkattr*( ) are as follows:

dm_sessid_t *sid* (I)
: The identifier for the session of interest.

void **hanp* (I)
: The handle for the file system. Information on all allocated files is returned; unallocated inodes are skipped.

size_t *hlen* (I)
: The length of the handle in bytes.

dm_token_t *token* (I)
: The token referencing the access right for the handle. The access right must be at least DM_RIGHT_SHARED or the token DM_NO_TOKEN may be used and the interface acquires the appropriate rights.

u_int *mask* (I)
: The *mask* argument controls which fields in the **dm_stat** structure should be returned. The mask is constructed by OR-ing together one or more of the following flags:

  DM_AT_HANDLE
  : The file's handle is returned.

  DM_AT_EMASK
  : The file's persistent event mask is returned.

  DM_AT_PMANR
  : A boolean (DM_TRUE or DM_FALSE) is returned indicating whether the file has persistent managed regions.

  DM_AT_PATTR
  : A boolean (DM_TRUE or DM_FALSE) is returned indicating whether the file has persistent data management attributes.

  DM_AT_DTIME
  : The time stamp of the persistent attributes if associated with the file.

DM_AT_CFLAG
The file change indicator is returned.

DM_AT_STAT
The file's general attributes as defined by the Single UNIX Specification **struct**stat.

dm_attrloc_t **locp* (I/O)
This is an offset, which is opaque to the calling DM application, that can be used by the DMAPI implementation to indicate the location in the object. It should not be modified by the DM application. It must be initialized via *dm_init_attrloc*( ) before calling *dm_get_bulkattr*( ), *dm_get_bulkall*( ) or *dm_get_dirattrs*( ).

size_t *buflen* (I)
The size of the buffer, in bytes.

void **bufp* (O)
This is filled in with the **dm_stat** information for the file system.

size_t **rlenp* (O)
The size of the returned information.

The arguments to *dm_get_bulkall*( ) are identical to those for *dm_get_bulkattr*( ), with the addition of one argument to specify the attribute of interest:

dm_attrname_t **attrnamep* (I)
The DM attribute to be retrieved.

The arguments to *dm_get_dirattrs*( ) are identical to those for *dm_get_bulkattr*( ) with the exception of the specification of the file handle:

void **hanp* (I)
The handle for the directory. Information on all the files in the directory is returned. Subdirectories are not traversed. If a subdirectory is a mount point, *dm_get_dirattrs*( ) returns information on the underlying mounted-on subdirectory, not the new mount point.

RETURN VALUE

dm_get_bulkattr( ), *dm_get_bulkall*( ) and *dm_get_dirattrs*( ) return 1 to indicate success and more information maybe available, or zero to indicate success and no more information is available. -1 is returned on error, in which case the global *errno* is set to one of the following values:

[EACCES]
The access right referenced by the token for the handle is not at least DM_RIGHT_SHARED.

[EBADF]
The file handle does not refer to an existing or accessible object.

[EFAULT]
The system detected an invalid address in attempting to use an argument.

[EINVAL]
The argument *locp* or *mask* is not a valid value.

[EINVAL]
The argument *token* is not a valid token.

[EINVAL]
The file handle does not represent a directory or the file system object.

[EINVAL]
The session is not valid.

[EIO]
An attempt to read the attributes resulted in an I/O error.

[ENOMEM]
The DMAPI could not obtain the required resources to complete the call.

[ENOSYS]
The DMAPI does not support *dm_get_bulkall* ( ).

[EPERM]
The caller does not hold the appropriate privilege.

SEE ALSO

dm_get_allocinfo ( ), *dm_get_fileattr* ( ), *dm_init_attrloc* ( ).

NAME

dm_get_config — return DMAPI implementation details and limits

SYNOPSIS

```
int
dm_get_config(
    void            *hanp,
    size_t           hlen,
    dm_config_t      flagname,
    dm_size_t       *retvalp)
```

DESCRIPTION

The function *dm_get_config*( ) returns information specific to an implementation of the DMAPI.

void **hanp* (I)
A handle for any file on the file system or a handle for the file system.

size_t *hlen* (I)
The length of the handle in bytes.

dm_config_t *flagname* (I)
The argument *flagname* is an **enum** and may contain one of the following values:

DM_CONFIG_BULKALL
A boolean value indicating whether the DMAPI implementation supports the *dm_get_bulkall*( ) function.

DM_CONFIG_CREATE_BY_HANDLE
A boolean value indicating whether the DMAPI implementation supports the *dm_create_by_handle*( ), *dm_mkdir_by_handle*( ) and *dm_symlink_by_handle*( ) functions.

DM_CONFIG_DTIME_OVERLOAD
A boolean value that indicates whether the *ctime* and *dtime* fields in the **dm_stat** structure share the same storage.

DM_CONFIG_LEGACY
A boolean value indicating whether the DMAPI implementation supports the *dm_make_handle*( ), *dm_make_fshandle*( ), *dm_handle_to_fshandle*( ), *dm_handle_to_igen*( ) and *dm_handle_to_ino*( ) legacy functions.

DM_CONFIG_LOCK_UPGRADE
A boolean value indicating whether the DMAPI implementation does or does not support upgrading/downgrading rights in non-blocking fashion without releasing the current right.

DM_CONFIG_MAX_ATTR_ON_DESTROY
The maximum number of bytes returned for the attribute *copy* field within a *destroy* event message. A size of 0 is returned if this feature is not supported by the implementation.

DM_CONFIG_MAX_ATTRIBUTE_SIZE
The maximum size in bytes per file that a single persistent attribute can occupy is returned. This is the size of the attribute data only.

DM_CONFIG_MAX_HANDLE_SIZE
The maximum size of handles in the file system. A size of 0 means it is unknown.

DM_CONFIG_MAX_MANAGED_REGIONS
The maximum number of managed regions supported per file is returned.

DM_CONFIG_MAX_MESSAGE_DATA
The number of bytes of data in the largest user-created event message. DM applications can use this value to determine the largest buffer size allowed in calls to *dm_create_userevent*( ) and *dm_send_msg*( )).

DM_CONFIG_OBJ_REF
A boolean value indicating whether the DMAPI implementation supports the *dm_obj_xxx*( ) functions.

DM_CONFIG_PENDING
A boolean value indicating whether the DMAPI implementation supports the *dm_pending*( ) function.

DM_CONFIG_PERS_ATTRIBUTES
A boolean value indicating whether the file system does or does not support persistent, opaque data management attributes.

DM_CONFIG_PERS_EVENTS
A boolean value is returned which indicates whether the DMAPI implementation supports support persistent event masks.

DM_CONFIG_PERS_INHERIT_ATTRIBS
A boolean value indicating whether the file system does or does not support inherited opaque data management attributes.

DM_CONFIG_PERS_MANAGED_REGIONS
A boolean value is returned that indicates whether the DMAPI implementation supports or does not support persistent managed regions.

DM_CONFIG_PUNCH_HOLE
A boolean value indicating whether the file system does or does not support punching holes (see *dm_punch/probe_hole*( ) on page 132).

DM_CONFIG_TOTAL_ATTRIBUTE_SPACE
The total available space per file for the storage of all persistent data management attributes, in bytes.

DM_CONFIG_WILL_RETRY
A boolean value is returned that indicates whether the DMAPI implementation retries the operation that caused a *nospace* event to be generated if a DM_RESP_CONTINUE response is returned.

For boolean values, a DM_TRUE return value indicates that the property is supported, while DM_FALSE indicates that the property is not supported. Other return values are dependent on the value of the flagname argument.

dm_size_t **retvalp* (O)
The value of the requested flag if the call succeeds. If *dm_get_config*( ) returns -1, the value is undefined.

RETURN VALUE

Zero is returned on success. On error, -1 is returned, and the global *errno* is set to one of the following values:

[EBADF]
The file handle does not refer to an existing or accessible object.

[EFAULT]
The system detected an invalid address in attempting to use an argument.

[EINVAL]
The argument flag_name does not contain a valid option.

[EPERM]
The caller does not hold the appropriate privilege.

SEE ALSO

dm_punch_hole( ), *dm_get_allocinfo* ( ).

NAME

dm_get_config_events — get a list of all events supported by the DMAPI implementation

SYNOPSIS

```
int
dm_get_config_events(
    void              *hanp,
    size_t             hlen,
    u_int              nelem,
    dm_eventset_t     *eventsetp,
    u_int             *nelemp)
```

DESCRIPTION

Return the list of supported events for a specific file system. The object can be either a regular file or the file system object. The returned event list is the set of all supported events in the file system containing the object. DM applications can use the DMEV_ISSET macro to determine if a specific event is supported.

void **hanp* (I)
: The handle for an object in the file system or a file system handle.

size_t *hlen* (I)
: The length of the handle in bytes.

u_int *nelem* (I)
: The number of elements in the event set array.

dm_eventset_t **eventsetp* (O)
: Buffer to be filled in with the list of supported events.

u_int **nelemp* (O)
: The number of elements read. If the buffer is not large enough to hold the requested information (as determined by the *nelem* parameter), then no data is copied, the call fails with [E2BIG], and *nelemp* is set to the number of elements that are available. *nelemp* is updated if either the call was successful or the call fails with [E2BIG], but is undefined otherwise.

RETURN VALUE

Zero is returned on success. On error, -1 is returned, and the global *errno* is set to one of the following values:

[E2BIG]
: The information is too large to fit into the buffer.

[EBADF]
: The handle does not refer to an existing or accessible object.

[EFAULT]
: The system detected an invalid address in attempting to use an argument.

[EPERM]
: The caller does not hold the appropriate privilege.

SEE ALSO

dm_get_events( ).

NAME

dm_get_dmattr — retrieve a data management attribute

SYNOPSIS

```
int
dm_get_dmattr(
    dm_sessid_t       sid,
    void             *hanp,
    size_t            hlen,
    dm_token_t        token,
    dm_attrname_t    *attrnamep,
    size_t            buflen,
    void             *bufp,
    size_t           *rlenp)
```

DESCRIPTION

The *dm_get_dmattr*( ) function retrieves a single, specific data management attribute for a file. The file's attribute time stamp is not altered.

dm_sessid_t *sid* (I)
: The identifier for the session of interest.

void **hanp* (I)
: The handle for the file for which the attributes should be retrieved.

size_t *hlen* (I)
: The length of the handle in bytes.

dm_token_t *token* (I)
: The token referencing the access right for the handle. The access right must be at least DM_RIGHT_SHARED, or the token DM_NO_TOKEN may be used and the interface acquires the appropriate rights.

dm_attrname_t **attrnamep* (I)
: The attribute to be retrieved.

size_t *buflen* (I)
: The size of the buffer in bytes.

void **bufp* (O)
: The buffer to be filled in with the value of the specified attribute's data.

size_t **rlenp* (O)
: The size of the requested information. If the buffer is not large enough to hold the requested information (as indicated by the *buflen* parameter), then no data is copied, the call fails with [E2BIG], and *rlenp* is set to the required size. *rlenp* is updated if either the call was successful or the call fails with [E2BIG], but is undefined otherwise.

RETURN VALUE

Zero is returned on success. On error, -1 is returned, and the global *errno* is set to one of the following values:

[E2BIG]
: The information is too large to fit into the buffer.

[EACCES]
: The access right referenced by the token for the handle is not at least DM_RIGHT_SHARED.

[EBADF]
The file handle does not refer to an existing or accessible object.

[EFAULT]
The system detected an invalid address in attempting to use an argument.

[EINVAL]
The argument token is not a valid token.

[EINVAL]
The session is not valid.

[ENOENT]
The attribute was not found.

[ENOMEM]
The DMAPI could not acquire the required resources to complete the call.

[ENOSYS]
The DMAPI implementation does not support this optional function.

[EIO]
An attempt to read the attribute resulted in an I/O error.

[EPERM]
The caller does not hold the appropriate privilege.

SEE ALSO

dm_set_dmattr( ), *dm_remove_dmattr*( ), *dm_getall_dmattr*( ).

NOTES

dm_get_dmattr( ) is an optional component of the DMAPI.

NAME

dm_get_eventlist — get the list of enabled events for an object

SYNOPSIS

```
int
dm_get_eventlist(
    dm_sessid_t        sid,
    void              *hanp,
    size_t             hlen,
    dm_token_t         token,
    u_int              nelem,
    dm_eventset_t     *eventsetp,
    u_int             *nelemp)
```

DESCRIPTION

Return the list of enabled events for the specified object. The object can be either a regular file or the file system object. The returned event list is the set of all events for the object. DM applications can use the DMEV_ISSET macro to determine if a specific event is enabled.

For DMAPI implementations that do not store event lists persistently and support the debut event, *dm_get_eventlist*( ) returns only those events that have been set via *dm_set_eventlist*( ) since the most recent debut event. The function does not itself cause a debut event to be generated.

The synchronous managed region events are set via the *dm_set_region*( ) interface. If there are any managed regions that have any events set (as determined by the *rg_flags* field in the struct B dm_region), *dm_get_eventlist*( ) returns the union of all of those flags fields.

dm_sessid_t *sid* (I)
: The identifier for the session of interest.

void **hanp* (I)
: The handle for the object.

size_t *hlen* (I)
: The length of the handle in bytes.

dm_token_t *token* (I)
: The token referencing the access right for the handle. The access right must be at least DM_RIGHT_SHARED or the token DM_NO_TOKEN may be used and the interface acquires the appropriate rights.

u_int *nelem* (I)
: The number of elements in the event set array.

dm_eventset_t **eventsetp* (O)
: Buffer to be filled in with the list of events.

u_int **nelemp* (O)
: The number of elements read. If the buffer is not large enough to hold the requested information (as determined by the *nelem* parameter), then no data is copied, the call fails with [E2BIG], and *nelemp* is set to the number of elements that are available. *nelemp* is updated if either the call was successful or the call fails with [E2BIG], but is undefined otherwise.

RETURN VALUE

Zero is returned on success. On error, -1 is returned, and the global *errno* is set to one of the following values:

[E2BIG]
The information is too large to fit into the buffer.

[EACCES]
The access right referenced by the token for the handle is not at least DM_RIGHT_SHARED.

[EBADF]
The handle does not refer to an existing or accessible object.

[EFAULT]
The system detected an invalid address in attempting to use an argument.

[EINVAL]
The argument token is not a valid token.

[EINVAL]
The session is not valid.

[ENOMEM]
The DMAPI could not obtain the required resources to complete the call.

[EPERM]
The caller does not hold the appropriate privilege.

SEE ALSO

dm_set_eventlist( ), *dm_set_disp*( ), *dm_get_events*( ), macro DMEV_ISSET.

NAME

dm_get_events — get the next available event messages

SYNOPSIS

```
int
dm_get_events(
    dm_sessid_t     sid,
    u_int           maxmsgs,
    u_int           flags,
    size_t          buflen,
    void           *bufp,
    size_t         *rlenp)
```

DESCRIPTION

Get the next event or events for a session. The event message is copied to the message buffer and includes both the common and event-specific fields of the event.

Messages can be retrieved in bulk; up to *maxmsgs* can be copied to the output buffer, provided that enough space is available. If no messages are immediately available, and the DM_EV_WAIT flag is set in the *flags* argument, then the calling process blocks interruptibly.

dm_sessid_t *sid* (I)
: The identifier for the session of interest.

u_int *maxmsgs* (I)
: The maximum number of messages that should be transferred in a single call. A value of zero indicates return all available messages that fit into the message buffer.

u_int *flags* (I)
: If the DM_EV_WAIT flag is not set and no messages are available, the calling process returns with [EAGAIN]. If DM_EV_WAIT is set and no messages are available, the calling process blocks interruptibly, waiting for messages to be enqueued on the session.

size_t *buflen* (I)
: The size of the message buffer in bytes. It must be large enough to hold at least one maximum sized event message.

void **bufp* (O)
: The message buffer to be filled in with one or more **dm_eventmsg** structures.

size_t *rlenp* (O)
: The size of the requested information. If the buffer is not large enough to hold the requested information (as indicated by the *buflen* parameter), then no data is copied, the call fails with [E2BIG], and *rlenp* is set to the required size. *rlenp* is updated if either the call was successful or the call fails with [E2BIG], but is undefined otherwise.

RETURN VALUE

Zero indicates success. On error, -1 is returned and the global *errno* is set to indicate the error.

[E2BIG]
: The information is too large to fit into the buffer.

[EAGAIN]
: The flags parameter had the DM_EV_WAIT flag set, and no messages are immediately available.

[EFAULT]
: The system detected an invalid address in attempting to use an argument.

[EINVAL]
The session is not valid.

[EINTR]
The process was blocked waiting for messages and was interrupted.

[ENOMEM]
The DMAPI could not obtain the required resources to complete the call.

[EPERM]
The caller does not hold the appropriate privilege.

SEE ALSO

dm_set_eventlist( ), *dm_set_disp*( ).

NAME

dm_get_fileattr — return file attributes

SYNOPSIS

```
int
dm_get_fileattr(
    dm_sessid_t     sid,
    void           *hanp,
    size_t          hlen,
    dm_token_t      token,
    u_int           mask,
    dm_stat_t      *statp)
```

DESCRIPTION

The function *dm_get_fileattr*( ) retrieves both standard file attributes and DM specific file attributes for the file specified by handle.

dm_sessid_t *sid* (I)
The identifier for the session of interest.

void **hanp* (I)
The handle for the file for which the file attributes should be retrieved.

size_t *hlen* (I)
The length of the handle in bytes.

dm_token_t *token* (I)
The token referencing the access right for the handle. The access right must be at least DM_RIGHT_SHARED, or the token DM_NO_TOKEN may be used and the interface acquires the appropriate rights.

u_int *mask* (I)
The argument *mask* indicates which fields of the **dm_stat** structure to return. The mask is constructed by OR-ing together one or more of the following flags:

DM_AT_EMASK
The file's persistent event mask is returned.

DM_AT_PMANR
A boolean (DM_TRUE or DM_FALSE) is returned indicating whether the file has persistent managed regions.

DM_AT_PATTR
A boolean (DM_TRUE or DM_FALSE) is returned indicating whether the file has persistent data management attributes.

DM_AT_DTIME
The time stamp of the persistent attributes if associated with the file.

DM_AT_CFLAG
The file change indicator is returned.

DM_AT_STAT
The file's general attributes as defined by the Single UNIX Specification struct **stat**.

dm_stat_t **statp* (O)
The buffer to be filled in with the required information. For fields that were not specified by the *mask* input value, the values of the corresponding field are not defined.

RETURN VALUE

Zero is returned on sucess. On error, -1 is returned, and the global *errno* is set to one of the following values:

[EACCES]
The access right referenced by the token for the handle is not at least DM_RIGHT_SHARED.

[EBADF]
The file handle does not refer to an existing or accessible object.

[EFAULT]
The system detected an invalid address in attempting to use an argument.

[EINVAL]
The argument *mask* is not valid.

[EINVAL]
The argument *token* is not a valid token.

[EINVAL]
The session is not valid.

[EIO]
An attempt to read the attributes resulted in an I/O error.

[ENOMEM]
The DMAPI could not obtain the required resources to complete the call.

[EPERM]
The caller does not hold the appropriate privilege.

SEE ALSO

dm_get_allocinfo( ), *dm_get_bulkattr*( ), *dm_get_dirattr*( ).

NAME

dm_get_mountinfo — return the information that was delivered on a mount event

SYNOPSIS

```
int
dm_get_mountinfo(
    dm_sessid_t    sid,
    void          *hanp,
    size_t         hlen,
    dm_token_t     token,
    size_t         buflen,
    void          *bufp,
    size_t        *rlenp)
```

DESCRIPTION

During initialization and often during recovery, DM applications need to get information about the file systems they are operating on. To facilitate this, *dm_get_mountinfo*( ) provides the same information that was originally generated on a mount event. This information is most likely kept in a static area in the DMAPI implementation; thus it is not a large burden on the implementation to return it both in a message and via this interface.

dm_sessid_t *sid* (I)
: The identifier for the session of interest.

void **hanp* (I)
: The handle for the file system meta-object.

size_t *hlen* (I)
: The length of the handle in bytes.

dm_token_t *token* (I)
: The token referencing the access right for the handle. The access right must be at least DM_RIGHT_SHARED, or the token DM_NO_TOKEN may be used and the interface acquires the appropriate rights.

size_t *buflen* (I)
: The length of the input buffer in bytes.

void **bufp* (O)
: A pointer to a buffer that is to be filled in with the information. The buffer should point to a **dm_mount_event** structure.

size_t *rlenp* (O)
: The size of the requested information. If the buffer is not large enough to hold the requested information (as indicated by the *buflen* parameter), then no data is copied, the call fails with [E2BIG], and *rlenp* is set to the required size. *rlenp* is updated if either the call was successful or the call fails with [E2BIG], but is undefined otherwise.

RETURN VALUE

Zero is returned on success. On error, -1 is returned, and the global *errno* is set to one of the following values:

[E2BIG]
: The buffer is not large enough to hold the requested information.

[EBADF]
: The handle does not refer to an existing or accessible object.

[EFAULT]
The system detected an invalid address in attempting to use an argument.

[EINVAL]
The handle is not a file system handle.

[EINVAL]
The session is not valid.

[EIO]
An attempt to read the mount information resulted in an I/O error.

[ENOMEM]
The DMAPI could not obtain the required resources to complete the call.

[EPERM]
The caller does not hold the appropriate privilege.

SEE ALSO

mount event.

NAME

dm_get_region — get the managed regions for a file

SYNOPSIS

```
int
dm_get_region(
    dm_sessid_t    sid,
    void          *hanp,
    size_t         hlen,
    dm_token_t     token,
    u_int          nelem,
    dm_region_t   *regbufp,
    u_int         *nelemp)
```

DESCRIPTION

Get the set of managed regions for a file.

dm_sessid_t *sid* (I)
The identifier for the session of interest.

void **hanp* (I)
The handle for the regular file.

size_t *hlen* (I)
The length of the handle in bytes.

dm_token_t *token* (I)
The token referencing the access right for the handle. The access right must be at least DM_RIGHT_SHARED, or the token DM_NO_TOKEN may be used and the interface acquires the appropriate rights.

u_int *nelem* (I)
The number of elements in the region buffer.

dm_region_t **regbufp* (O)
A pointer to the structure defining the regions to be filled in.

u_int **nelemp* (O)
The number of elements read. If the buffer is not large enough to hold the requested information (as determined by the *nelem* parameter), then no data is copied, the call fails with [E2BIG], and *nelemp* is set to the number of elements that are available. *nelemp* is updated if either the call was successful or the call fails with [E2BIG], but is undefined otherwise.

RETURN VALUES

Zero is returned on success. On error, -1 is returned, and the global *errno* is set to one of the following values:

[E2BIG]
The information is too large to fit into the buffer.

[EACCES]
The access right referenced by the token for the handle is not at least DM_RIGHT_SHARED.

[EBADF]
The file handle does not refer to an existing or accessible object.

[EFAULT]
The system detected an invalid address in attempting to use an argument.

[EINVAL]
The handle does not refer to a regular file.

[EINVAL]
The session is not valid.

[EINVAL]
The argument token is not a valid token.

[ENOMEM]
The DMAPI could not acquire the required resources to complete the call. LI "[EPERM]"
The caller does not hold the appropriate privilege.

SEE ALSO

dm_set_region( ).

NAME

dm_getall_disp — get disposition of events for all file systems for a session

SYNOPSIS

```
int
dm_getall_disp(
    dm_sessid_t     sid,
    size_t          buflen,
    void           *bufp,
    size_t         *rlenp)
```

DESCRIPTION

Get the set of all dispositions of events for all file systems for the indicated session. Since a session may be receiving events on more than one file system, *dm_getall_disp*( ) returns the disposition of events for every file system that was specified in a *dm_set_disp*( ) function.

dm_sessid_t *sid* (I)
: The identifier for the session of interest.

size_t *buflen* (I)
: The length of the input buffer in bytes.

void **bufp* (O)
: The buffer to be filled in with **dm_dispinfo** structures.

size_t **rlenp* (O)
: The size of the requested information. If the buffer is not large enough to hold the requested information (as indicated by the *buflen* parameter), then no data is copied, the call fails with [E2BIG], and *rlenp* is set to the required size. *rlenp* is updated if either the call was successful or the call fails with [E2BIG], but is undefined otherwise.

RETURN VALUE

Zero is returned on success. On error, -1 is returned, and the global *errno* is set to one of the following values:

[E2BIG]
: The information is too large to fit into the buffer.

[EFAULT]
: The system detected an invalid address in attempting to use an argument.

[EINVAL]
: The session is not valid.

[ENOMEM]
: The DMAPI could not acquire the required resources to complete the call.

[EPERM]
: he caller does not hold the appropriate privilege.

SEE ALSO

dm_set_disp( ).

NAME

dm_getall_dmattr — retrieve all of a file's data management attributes

SYNOPSIS

```
int
dm_getall_dmattr(
    dm_sessid_t     sid,
    void           *hanp,
    size_t          hlen,
    dm_token_t      token,
    size_t          buflen,
    void           *bufp,
    size_t         *rlenp)
```

DESCRIPTION

The *dm_getall_dmattr*( ) function returns all the attributes and attribute data associated with the specified file system object.

dm_sessid_t *sid* (I)
: The identifier for the session of interest.

void **hanp* (I)
: The handle for the file for which the attributes should be retrieved.

size_t *hlen* (I)
: The length of the handle in bytes.

dm_token_t *token* (I)
: The token referencing the access right for the handle. The access right must be at least DM_RIGHT_SHARED or the token DM_NO_TOKEN may be used and the interface acquires the appropriate rights.

size_t *buflen* (I)
: The size of the buffer in bytes.

void **bufp* (O)
: The buffer to be filled in with **dm_attrlist** structures.

size_t **rlenp* (O)
: The size of the requested information. If the buffer is not large enough to hold the requested information (as indicated by the *buflen* parameter), then no data is copied, the call fails with [E2BIG], and *rlenp* is set to the required size. *rlenp* is updated if either the call was successful or the call fails with [E2BIG], but is undefined otherwise.

RETURN VALUE

Zero is returned on success. On error, -1 is returned, and the global *errno* is set to one of the following values:

[E2BIG]
: The information is too large to fit into the buffer.

[EACCES]
: The access right referenced by the token for the handle is not at least DM_RIGHT_SHARED.

[EBADF]
: The file handle does not refer to an existing or accessible object.

[EFAULT]
: The system detected an invalid address in attempting to use an argument.

[EINVAL]
The argument token is not a valid token.

[EINVAL]
The session is not valid.

[EIO]
An attempt to read the attributes resulted in an I/O error.

[ENOMEM]
The DMAPI could not acquire the required resources to complete the call.

[ENOSYS]
The DMAPI implementation does not support this optional function.

[EPERM]
The caller does not hold the appropriate privilege.

SEE ALSO

dm_get_dmattr( ), *dm_attrlist_t*( ).

NOTES

dm_getall_dmattr( ) is an optional component of the DMAPI.

dm_getall_inherit( )

NAME

dm_getall_inherit — get all inheritable attributes for the specified file system

SYNOPSIS

```
int
dm_getall_inherit(
    dm_sessid_t      sid,
    void            *hanp,
    size_t           hlen,
    dm_token_t       token,
    u_int            nelem,
    dm_inherit_t     inheritbufp,
    u_int           *nelemp)
```

DESCRIPTION

The *dm_getall_inherit*( ) function returns a list of all inheritable attributes associated with the given file system object. The inheritability property of attributes is not persistent across reboots. The attributes are returned in a **dm_inherit** structure, which gives the attribute name and the file type that the attribute applies to.

dm_sessid_t *sid* (I)
: The identifier for the session of interest.

void **hanp* (I)
: The file system handle.

size_t *hlen* (I)
: The length of the handle in bytes.

dm_token_t *token* (I)
: The token referencing the access right for the handle. The access right must be at least DM_RIGHT_SHARED or the token DM_NO_TOKEN may be used and the interface acquires the appropriate rights.

u_int *nelem* (I)
: The number of elements to return. No more than nelem is returned.

dm_inherit_t **inheritbufp* (O)
: The buffer to be filled with inheritable attributes.

u_int **nelemp* (O)
: The number of elements read. If the buffer is not large enough to hold the requested information (as determined by the *nelem* parameter), then no data is copied, the call fails with [E2BIG], and *nelemp* is set to the number of elements that are available. *nelemp* is updated if either the call was successful or the call fails with [E2BIG], but is undefined otherwise.

RETURN VALUE

Zero is returned on success. On error, -1 is returned, and the global *errno* is set to one of the following values:

[E2BIG]
: The information is too large to fit into the buffer.

[EACCES]
: The access right referenced by the token for the handle is not at least DM_RIGHT_SHARED.

[EBADF]
: The file handle does not refer to an existing or accessible object.

[EFAULT]
The system detected an invalid address in attempting to use an argument.

[EINVAL]
The argument *token* is not a valid token.

[EINVAL]
The handle is not a file system handle.

[EINVAL]
The session is not valid.

[EIO]
An attempt to read the attributes resulted in an I/O error.

[ENOSYS]
The DMAPI implementation does not support this optional function.

[EPERM]
The caller does not hold the appropriate privilege.

SEE ALSO

dm_set_inherit( ), *dm_clear_inherit*( ), *dm_inherit_t*.

NOTES

dm_getall_inherit( ) is an optional component of the DMAPI.

NAME

dm_getall_sessions — get all extant sessions

SYNOPSIS

```
int
dm_getall_sessions(
    u_int           nelem,
    dm_sessid_t    *sidbufp,
    u_int          *nelemp)
```

DESCRIPTION

The *dm_getall_sessions*( ) function returns a list of all the sessions that exist on a system.

u_int *nelem* (I)
The maximum number of elements to return.

dm_sessid_t **sidbufp* (O)
The buffer where the active sessions are to be deposited.

u_int **nelemp* (O)
The number of elements read. If the buffer is not large enough to hold the requested information (as determined by the *nelem* parameter), then no data is copied, the call fails with [E2BIG], and *nelemp* is set to the number of elements that are available. *nelemp* is updated if either the call was successful or the call fails with [E2BIG], but is undefined otherwise.

RETURN VALUE

Zero is returned on success. On error, -1 is returned, and the global *errno* is set to one of the following values:

[E2BIG]
The information is too large to fit into the buffer.

[EFAULT]
The system detected an invalid address in attempting to use an argument.

[ENOMEM]
The DMAPI could not obtain the required resources to complete the call.

[EPERM]
The caller does not hold the appropriate privilege.

SEE ALSO

dm_find_eventmsg( ), *dm_create_session*( ), *dm_getall_tokens*( ), *dm_query_session*( ).

NAME

dm_getall_tokens — get all outstanding tokens for a session

SYNOPSIS

```
int
dm_getall_tokens(
        dm_sessid_t     sid,
        u_int           nelem,
        dm_token_t     *tokenbufp,
        u_int          *nelemp)
```

DESCRIPTION

This gets all the outstanding tokens that are associated with a session. An outstanding token is a token that corresponds to a synchronous message that has been delivered but not responded to. User event messages created with *dm_create_userevent*( ) are implicitly synchronous, and if tokens exist for these messages, they are also returned.

dm_sessid_t *sid* (I)
The identifier for the session of interest.

u_int *nelem* (I)
The maximum number of elements to return.

dm_token_t **tokenbufp* (O)
The buffer that should be filled in with all outstanding tokens.

u_int **nelemp* (O)
The number of elements read. If the buffer is not large enough to hold the requested information (as determined by the *nelem* parameter), then no data is copied, the call fails with [E2BIG], and *nelemp* is set to the number of elements that are available. *nelemp* is updated if either the call was successful or the call fails with [E2BIG], but is undefined otherwise.

RETURN VALUE

Zero is returned on success. On error, -1 is returned, and the global *errno* is set to one of the following values:

[E2BIG]
The information is too large to fit into the buffer.

[EFAULT]
The system detected an invalid address in attempting to use an argument.

[EINVAL]
The session is not valid.

[ENOMEM]
The DMAPI could not obtain the required resources to complete the call.

[EPERM]
The caller does not hold the appropriate privilege.

SEE ALSO

dm_getall_sessions( ), *dm_find_eventmsg*( ), *dm_respond_event*( ), *dm_create_session*( ).

dm_handle_cmp( )

NAME

dm_handle_cmp — file handle comparison

SYNOPSIS

```
int
dm_handle_cmp(
        void        *hanp1,
        size_t       hlen1,
        void        *hanp2,
        size_t       hlen2)
```

DESCRIPTION

Compare two handles for equality.

void **hanp1* (I)
The first handle to compare.

size_t *hlen1* (I)
The length of the first handle in bytes.

void **hanp2* (I)
The second handle to compare.

size_t *hlen2* (I)
The length of the second handle in bytes.

RETURN VALUE

<0 *hanp1* is less than *hanp2* (according to an implementation defined rule).

=0 *hanp1* and *hanp2* represent the same object.

>0 *hanp1* is greater than *hanp2* (according to an implementation defined rule).

The rationale behind multiple return values is so that DM applications can use *dm_handle_cmp*( ) in sorting.

NAME

dm_handle_hash — hashes the contents of a handle

SYNOPSIS

```
u_int
dm_handle_hash(
    void      *hanp,
    size_t     hlen)
```

DESCRIPTION

Hashes the contents of a handle and returns the hashed value.

void **hanp* (I)
  A pointer to a handle.

size_t *hlen* (I)
  The length of the handle in bytes.

RETURN VALUE

Returns a value derived in an implementation defined manner from the contents of the handle. *dm_handle_hash*( ) has no failure indication.

dm_handle_is_valid( )

NAME

dm_handle_is_valid — determine if a handle is valid

SYNOPSIS

```
dm_boolean_t
dm_handle_is_valid(
    void        *hanp,
    size_t       hlen)
```

DESCRIPTION

Determine if a handle is valid.

void *hanp* (I)
: The handle to check for validity.

size_t *hlen* (I)
: The length of the handle.

RETURN VALUE

DM_TRUE
: The handle is valid.

DM_FALSE
: The handle is not a valid DM handle.

NAME

dm_handle_to_fshandle — obtain the file system handle corresponding to an object handle

SYNOPSIS

```
int
dm_handle_to_fshandle(
    void       *hanp,
    size_t      hlen,
    void      **fshanpp,
    size_t     *fshlenp)
```

DESCRIPTION

The *dm_handle_to_fshandle*( ) function obtains the handle for the file system in which the object handle resides. *hanp* may not be a file system handle or the global handle.

void **hanp* (I)
: The object handle.

size_t *hlen* (I)
: The length of the handle in bytes.

void ***fshanpp* (O)
: A pointer that is set to point to the file system handle.

size_t **fshlenp* (O)
: The length of the file system handle in bytes.

RETURN VALUE

Zero is returned on success. On error, -1 is returned, and the global *errno* is set to one of the following values:

[EBADF]
: *hanp* does not refer to an existing or accessible object.

[EFAULT]
: The system detected an invalid address in attempting to use an argument.

[ENOMEM]
: The DMAPI could not obtain the required resources to complete the call.

[EPERM]
: The caller does not hold the appropriate privilege.

dm_handle_to_path( )

NAME

dm_handle_to_path — get a path name

SYNOPSIS

```
int
dm_handle_to_path(
    void     *dirhanp,
    size_t    dirhlen,
    void     *targhanp,
    size_t    targhlen,
    size_t    buflen,
    char     *pathbufp,
    size_t   *rlenp)
```

DESCRIPTION

Takes two object handles, one of which must be the handle of a directory containing the file identified by the other handle, and constructs a path name. If the first character of the path is "/", then the path is an absolute path name, otherwise it is relative to the containing file system.

void **dirhanp* (I)
: A handle for the directory containing the target file.

size_t *dirhlen* (I)
: The length of the directory handle in bytes.

void **targhanp* (I)
: A file handle for the target file. The target file must be in the directory represented by *dirhanp*.

size_t *targhlen* (I)
: The length of the target handle in bytes.

size_t *buflen* (I)
: The length of the path name buffer in bytes.

char **pathbufp* (O)
: The buffer for the path name.

size_t **rlenp* (O)
: Always updated if the call is successful and undefined if [E2BIG] is returned.

RETURN VALUE

Zero is returned on success. On error, -1 is returned, and the global *errno* is set to one of the following values:

[E2BIG]
: The information is too large to fit into the buffer.

[EBADF]
: Either *dirhanp* or *targhanp* does not refer to an existing or accessible object.

[EFAULT]
: The system detected an invalid address in attempting to use an argument.

[ENOMEM]
: The DMAPI could not obtain the required resources to complete the call.

[EPERM]
: The caller does not hold the appropriate privilege.

NAME

dm_init_attrloc — initialize a bulk attribute location offset

SYNOPSIS

```
int
dm_init_attrloc(
    dm_sessid_t      sid,
    void            *hanp,
    size_t           hlen,
    dm_token_t       token,
    dm_attrloc_t    *locp)
```

DESCRIPTION

The function *dm_init_attrloc*( ) initializes an opaque cookie for use by the functions *dm_get_bulkattr*( ), *dm_get_bulkall*( ) and *dm_get_dirattrs*( ).

The arguments to *dm_init_attrloc*( ) are as follows:

dm_sessid_t *sid* (I)
: The identifier for the session of interest.

void **hanp* (I)
: The handle for the file system or the directory.

size_t *hlen* (I)
: The length of the handle in bytes.

dm_token_t *token* (I)
: The token referencing the access right for the handle. The access right must be at least DM_RIGHT_SHARED or the token DM_NO_TOKEN may be used and the interface acquires the appropriate rights.

dm_attrloc_t **locp* (O)
: Pointer to an offset "cookie" to initialize.

RETURN VALUE

dm_init_attrloc( ) returns a value of zero upon successful completion. Otherwise a value of -1 is returned and *errno* is set to one of the following values:

[EACCES]
: The access right referenced by the token for the handle is not at least DM_RIGHT_SHARED.

[EBADF]
: The file handle does not refer to an existing or accessible object.

[EFAULT]
: The system detected an invalid address in attempting to use an argument.

[EINVAL]
: The argument *token* is not a valid token.

[EINVAL]
: The file handle does not represent a directory or the file system object.

[EINVAL]
: The session is not valid.

[EPERM]
: The caller does not hold the appropriate privilege.

SEE ALSO

dm_get_bulkattr( ), *dm_get_bulkall*( ), *dm_get_dirattr*( ).

NAME

dm_init_service — perform implementation-defined initialization

SYNOPSIS

```
int
dm_init_service(
    char    **versionstrpp)
```

DESCRIPTION

Each process that uses the DMAPI must call *dm_init_service*( ) before any other DMAPI function. This allows the implementation of the DMAPI to perform any required initialization. The *dm_init_service*( ) function returns a NULL terminated version string which is unique to an implementation and may be compared against DM_VER_STR_CONTENTS to verify at run-time that the DMAPI implementation which the DM application was compiled for is the one that is running.

The results of using any other DMAPI function are undefined if *dm_init_service*( ) is not called before other DMAPI functions.

RETURN VALUE

Zero is returned on success. On error, -1 is returned, and the global *errno* is set to one of the following values:

[ENOMEM]
: The DMAPI could not obtain the required resources to complete the call.

[ENOSYS]
: The DMAPI is not supported on this platform.

[EPERM]
: The caller does not hold the appropriate privilege.

NAME

dm_make_handle — construct DMAPI object handle
dm_make_fshandle — construct DMAPI file system handle
dm_handle_to_fsid — extract file system ID from handle
dm_handle_to_igen — extract inode generation count from handle
dm_handle_to_ino — extract inode from handle

SYNOPSIS

```
int
dm_make_handle(
    dm_fsid_t      *fsidp,
    dm_ino_t       *inop,
    dm_igen_t      *igenp,
    void          **hanpp,
    size_t         *hlenp)

int
dm_make_fshandle(
    dm_fsid_t      *fsid,
    void          **hanpp,
    size_t         *hlenp)

int
dm_handle_to_fsid(
    void           *hanp,
    size_t          hlen,
    dm_fsid_t      *fsidp)

int
dm_handle_to_igen(
    void           *hanp,
    size_t          hlen,
    dm_igen_t      *igenp)

int
dm_handle_to_ino(
    void           *hanp,
    size_t          hlen,
    dm_ino_t       *inop)
```

DESCRIPTION

This set of functions allows a DM application to compose and decompose DMAPI opaque handles. It is intended as a porting aid when upgrading legacy HSM applications to the DMAPI interface.

The *dm_make_handle*( ) function converts a file system ID, inode number, and inode generation count into a handle.

dm_fsid_t **fsidp* (I)
: The file system ID.

dm_ino_t **inop* (I)
: The inode number.

dm_igen_t **igenp* (I)
The inode generation count.

void ***hanpp* (O)
A pointer which is initialized by the DMAPI to point to a region of memory containing an opaque DM handle. The caller is responsible for freeing the allocated memory.

size_t **hlenp* (O)
The length of the handle in bytes.

The *dm_make_fshandle*( ) function converts a file system ID into a file system handle.

dm_fsid_t **fsidp* (I)
The file system ID.

void ***hanpp* (O)
A pointer which is initialized by the DMAPI to point to a region of memory containing an opaque DM handle. The caller is responsible for freeing the handle.

size_t **hlenp* (O)
The length of the handle in bytes.

The *dm_handle_to_fsid*( ) function extracts a file system ID from a handle.

void **hanp* (I)
A pointer to an opaque DM handle previously returned by DMAPI.

size_t *hlen* (I)
The length of the handle in bytes.

dm_fsid_t **fsidp* (O)
A pointer to the file system ID.

The *dm_handle_to_igen*( ) function extracts an inode generation count from a handle.

void **hanp* (I)
A pointer to an opaque DM handle previously returned by DMAPI.

size_t *hlen* (I)
The length of the handle in bytes.

dm_igen_t **igenp* (O)
A pointer to the inode generation count.

The *dm_handle_to_ino*( ) function extracts an inode number from a handle.

void **hanp* (I)
A pointer to an opaque DM handle previously returned by DMAPI.

size_t hlen (I)
The length of the handle in bytes.

dm_ino_t **inop* (O)
A pointer to the inode number.

RETURN VALUE

Zero is returned on success. On error, -1 is returned, and the global *errno* is set to one of the following values:

[EBADF]
The file handle does not refer to an existing or accessible object.

[EFAULT]
The system detected an invalid address in attempting to use an argument.

[EINVAL]
The argument *token* is not a valid token.

[ENOMEM]
The DMAPI could not obtain the required resources to complete the call.

[ENOSYS]
Function is not supported by the DM implementation.

[EPERM]
The caller does not hold the appropriate privilege.

SEE ALSO

dm_handle_free( ).

NOTES

dm_make_handle( ), *dm_make_fshandle*( ), *dm_handle_to_fsid*( ), *dm_handle_to_igen*( ) and *dm_handle_to_ino*( ) are optional components of the DMAPI.

NAME

dm_mkdir_by_handle — create a directory object using a handle

SYNOPSIS

```
int
dm_mkdir_by_handle(
    dm_sessid_t     sid,
    void           *dirhanp,
    size_t          dirhlen,
    dm_token_t      token,
    void           *hanp,
    size_t          hlen,
    char           *cname)
```

DESCRIPTION

dm_mkdir_by_handle( ) allows applications the ability to create a directory in a directory specified by *dirhanp* and with a component name specified by *cname* that can, after creation, be referenced by the supplied target handle *hanp*. This is useful when an application is reconstructing a directory for which it still has the data and attributes stored on alternate media.

It is the responsibility of the user of this function to reconstruct the object state, including extended attributes. See *dm_set_fileattr*( ) and *dm_set_dmattr*( ).

If an object cannot be constructed by the file system for the specified handle, an error is returned.

dm_sessid_t *sid* (I)
: The identifier for the session of interest.

void **dirhanp* (I)
: The handle for the directory that contains the target directory.

size_t *dirhlen* (I)
: The length of the directory handle in bytes.

dm_token_t *token* (I)
: The token referencing the access right for the parent directory handle. The access right must be at DM_RIGHT_EXCL or the token DM_NO_TOKEN may be used and the interface acquires the appropriate rights.

void **hanp* (I)
: The file handle of the directory.

size_t *hlen* (I)
: The length of the file handle in bytes.

char **cname* (I)
: The name of the directory to be created in the specified directory.

RETURN VALUE

Zero is returned on success. On error, -1 is returned, and the global *errno* is set to one of the following values:

[EACCES]
: The access right referenced by the token for the parent directory handle is not DM_RIGHT_EXCL.

[EBADF]
: The parent directory handle does not refer to an existing or accessible object.

[EEXIST]
The target directory handle refers to an existing object.

[EFAULT]
The system detected an invalid address in attempting to use an argument.

[EINVAL]
The argument *token* is not a valid token.

[EINVAL]
The session is not valid.

[EPERM]
The caller does not hold the appropriate privilege.

SEE ALSO

dm_set_fileattr( ), *dm_set_dmattr*( ), *dm_create_by_handle*( ), *dm_symlink_by_handle*( ).

NAME

dm_move_event — move an event from one session to another

SYNOPSIS

```
int
dm_move_event
    dm_sessid_t    srcsid,
    dm_token_t     token,
    dm_sessid_t    targetsid,
    dm_token_t    *rtokenp)
```

DESCRIPTION

The *dm_move_event*( ) function transfers an outstanding event message between sessions.

The event message remains outstanding, even though it is now enqueued on a different session. Once the call returns successfully, the old token that references the message is no longer valid. The token returned in *rtokenp* must be used in subsequent calls to reference the message.

dm_sessid_t *srcsid* (I)
: The source session identifier.

dm_token_t *token* (I)
: The token that identifies the message that is to be moved.

dm_sessid_t *targetsid* (I)
: The new session that is to receive the outstanding event.

dm_token_t **rtokenp* (O)
: The new token that must be used to refer to the message.

RETURN VALUE

Zero is returned on success. On error, -1 is returned, and the global *errno* is set to one of the following values:

[EFAULT]
: The system detected an invalid address in attempting to use an argument.

[EINVAL]
: The source or target sessions are not valid.

[ENOENT]
: There is no message corresponding to the token.

[ENOMEM]
: The DMAPI could not obtain the required resources to complete the call.

[EPERM]
: The caller does not hold the appropriate privilege.

SEE ALSO

dm_get_events( ), *dm_respond_event*( ).

dm_obj_ref_hold/release/query( )

NAME

dm_obj_ref_hold — place a hold on a file system object
dm_obj_ref_rele — release a hold on a file system object
dm_obj_ref_query — query for a hold on a file system object

SYNOPSIS

```
int
dm_obj_ref_hold(
    dm_sessid_t      sid,
    dm_token_t       token,
    void            *hanp,
    size_t           hlen)

int
dm_obj_ref_rele(
    dm_sessid_t      sid,
    dm_token_t       token,
    void            *hanp,
    size_t           hlen)

int
dm_obj_ref_query(
    dm_sessid_t      sid,
    dm_token_t       token,
    void            *hanp,
    size_t           hlen)
```

DESCRIPTION

This set of functions allows the DM application to place and release holds on file system objects. The effect is to prevent the object from being flushed out for the duration of the hold, thus no debut events will occur.

System behavior is undefined if an attempt is made to place multiple holds on the same handle/token pair. For portability, the DM application should issue a single hold/release, and use *dm_obj_ref_query*( ) to determine if a hold is already in place.

Creating the hold may cause a debut event to occur and responding to an event releases all holds associated with the event.

dm_sessid_t *sid* (I)
: The identifier for the session of interest.

dm_token_t *token* (I)
: The token referencing access rights for the specified object.

void **hanp* (I)
: The handle for the file system object for which a hold is being placed, released, or queried.

size_t *hlen* (I)
: The length of the handle in bytes.

RETURN VALUE

dm_obj_ref_hold( ) and *dm_obj_ref_rele*( ) return zero on success. *dm_obj_ref_query*( ) returns 1 if there is a hold currently associated with the specified object, session id, and token; it returns 0 if there is no hold. On error, -1 is returned and the global *errno* is set to one of the following values:

[EACCES]
The access right referenced by the token for the handle is not at least DM_RIGHT_SHARED.

[EBADF]
The file handle does not refer to an existing or accessible object.

[EBUSY]
There is a hold already in place for the specified object/token.

[EFAULT]
The system detected an invalid address in attempting to use an argument.

[EINVAL]
The argument ,I token is not a valid token.

[EINVAL]
The handle is not a file system handle.

[EINVAL]
The session is not valid.

[ENOMEM]
Insufficient memory to complete the call.

[ENOSYS]
Function is not supported by the DM implementation.

[EPERM]
The caller does not hold the appropriate privilege.

NOTES

The *dm_obj_ref_hold*( ), *dm_obj_ref_rele*( ) and *dm_obj_ref_query*( ) are optional components of the DMAPI.

NAME

dm_path_to_handle — create a file handle from a path name
dm_fd_to_handle — create a file handle from a file descriptor
dm_path_to_fshandle — create a file system handle from a path name
dm_handle_free — free the storage allocated for a handle

SYNOPSIS

```
int
dm_path_to_handle(
    char        *path,
    void       **hanpp,
    size_t      *hlenp)

int
dm_fd_to_handle(
    int          fd,
    void       **hanpp,
    size_t      *hlenp)

int
dm_path_to_fshandle(
    char        *path,
    void       **hanpp,
    size_t      *hlenp)

void
dm_handle_free(
    void        *hanp,
    size_t       hlen)
```

DESCRIPTION

This set of functions deals with file handles, which are opaque to a DM application. File handles uniquely identify an object.

dm_path_to_handle( ) converts a path name into a file handle. If the final component of the path name is a symbolic link, the file handle returned is for the symbolic link itself, and not for the object that the symbolic link references (if any).

char **path* (I)
The path name of the object.

void ***hanpp* (O)
A pointer that is initialized by the DMAPI to point to a region of memory containing an opaque DM handle. The caller is responsible for freeing the allocated memory.

size_t **hlenp* (O)
The length of the handle in bytes.

dm_fd_to_handle( ) converts a file descriptor into a file handle.

int *fd* (I)
A file descriptor to the object.

void ***hanpp* (O)
A pointer that is initialized by the DMAPI to point to a region of memory containing an opaque DM handle. The caller is responsible for freeing the allocated memory.

size_t **hlenp* (O)
The length of the handle in bytes.

dm_path_to_fshandle( ) returns the file system handle given a path name to any file in the file system. If the final component of the path name is a symbolic link, the file handle returned is the file system handle for the file system containing the symbolic link and not the file handle for the file system containing the object that the symbolic link references (if any). The file system handle is used by many DMAPI functions to identify a file system.

char **path* (I)
A path name to any file in the file system.

void ***hanpp* (O)
A pointer that is initialized by the DMAPI to point to a region of memory containing an opaque DM handle that represents the file system meta object. The caller is responsible for freeing the allocated memory.

size_t **hlenp* (O)
The length of the handle in bytes.

dm_handle_free( ) frees the storage allocated for a handle that was previously returned by *dm_path_to_handle*( ), *dm_fd_to_handle*( ), *dm_path_to_fshandle*( ), *dm_make_handle*( ), *dm_handle_to_fshandle*( ) or *dm_make_fshandle*( ).

void **hanp* (I) Pointer to the storage area for the file handle that should be freed.

size_t *hlen* (I) The length of the handle in bytes.

RETURN VALUE

dm_handle_free( ) has no failure indication. The other functions return zero is on success. On error, -1 is returned, and the global *errno* is set to one of the following values:

[EACCES]
Search permission is denied for a component of path.

[EBADF]
fd is not a valid open file descriptor.

[EFAULT]
The system detected an invalid address in attempting to use an argument.

[ELOOP]
Too many symbolic links were encountered in translating the path name.

[ENAMETOOLONG]
A component of path or the entire length of path exceeded the file system limits.

[ENOENT]
A component of path that must exist does not exist.

[ENOMEM]
Insufficient memory to allocate the file handle.

[ENOTDIR]
A component of the specified path name was not a directory when a directory was expected.

[ENXIO]
The file system containing the file opened on *fd* or the final component of path does not support the DMAPI.

[EPERM]
The caller does not hold the appropriate privilege.

NAME

dm_pending — notify FS of slow DM application operation

SYNOPSIS

```
int
dm_pending(
    dm_sessid_t         sid,
    dm_token_t          token,
    dm_timestruct_t    *delay)
```

DESCRIPTION

The *dm_pending*( ) function permits a DM application to notify the DMAPI implementation when it detects that an operation will take an unusually long time.

The function indicates that the response to the event identified by token is delayed for an approximate duration of delay. The value of delay is a hint only.

The *dm_pending*( ) function must be sent before *dm_respond_event*( ), and is not a replacement for *dm_respond_event*( ).

A DM application is not required to generate *dm_pending*( ) notifications, and the DMAPI implementation is free to use or ignore the information as it sees fit. Typical use for *dm_pending*( ) is to advise the underlying file system about the delay.

dm_sessid_t *sid* (I)
: The identifier for the session of interest.

dm_token_t *token* (I)
: The token representing the event that is expected to be delayed.

dm_timestruct_t **delay* (I)
: Expected duration of delay.

RETURN VALUE

Zero is returned on success. On error, -1 is returned, and the global *errno* is set to one of the following values:

[ENOSYS]
: Function is not supported by the DM implementation.

NOTES

The *dm_pending*( ) function is an optional component of the DMAPI.

NAME

dm_punch_hole — create a hole in a file
dm_probe_hole — return the rounded result of the area where a hole is to be punched

SYNOPSIS

```
int
dm_punch_hole(
    dm_sessid_t     sid,
    void           *hanp,
    size_t          hlen,
    dm_token_t      token,
    dm_off_t        off,
    dm_size_t       len)

int
dm_probe_hole(
    dm_sessid_t     sid,
    void           *hanp,
    size_t          hlen,
    dm_token_t      token,
    dm_off_t        off,
    dm_size_t       len,
    dm_off_t       *roffp,
    dm_size_t      *rlenp)
```

DESCRIPTION

The *dm_punch_hole*( ) function is used to make a hole in a regular file, logically writing zeroes to the designated area while bypassing normal DMAPI event generation. The DMAPI implementation may then optionally free media resources for that area. *dm_probe_hole*( ) is used to interrogate the DMAPI implementation for size and offset around the area where the hole is to be punched. The DMAPI implementation can impose boundary and rounding constraints within which the DM application must be willing to work.

The DMAPI guarantees that if the DM_RIGHT_EXCL access right is held across a call to *dm_probe_hole*( ), and then the returned results of the probe call are used to make a *dm_punch_hole*( ) call, the function will not fail because of rounding.

dm_punch_hole( ) takes the following arguments:

dm_sessid_t *sid* (I)
: The identifier for the session of interest.

void **hanp* (I)
: File handle for the regular file that should have its storage manipulated.

size_t *hlen* (I)
: The length of the handle in bytes.

dm_token_t *token* (I)
: The token referencing the access right for the handle. The access right must be DM_RIGHT_EXCL or the token DM_NO_TOKEN may be used and the interface acquires the appropriate rights.

dm_off_t *off* (I)
: The starting offset in the file to begin punching a hole. If the offset does not exactly match what the DMAPI implementation can support, [EAGAIN] is returned.

dm_size_t *len* (I)
The length of the hole to punch, in bytes. If the length does not exactly match what the DMAPI implementation can support, [EAGAIN] is returned. If zero is specified, hole is punched to the end of file.

dm_probe_hole( ) takes the following arguments:

dm_sessid_t *sid* (I)
The identifier for the session of interest.

void **hanp* (I)
File handle for the regular file that should have its storage manipulated.

size_t *hlen* (I)
The length of the handle in bytes.

dm_token_t *token* (I)
The token referencing the access right for the handle. The access right must be at least DM_RIGHT_SHARED or the token DM_NO_TOKEN may be used and the interface acquires the appropriate rights.

dm_off_t *off* (I)
The desired starting offset in the file for the hole.

dm_size_t *len* (I)
The desired length of the hole to punch, in bytes. A length of zero corresponds to the end of the file.

dm_off_t **roffp* (O)
The rounded starting offset of the hole that the DMAPI implementation supports.

dm_size_t **rlenp* (O)
The rounded length of the hole, in bytes, that the DMAPI implementation supports.

RETURN VALUE

Zero is returned on success. On error, -1 is returned, and the global *errno* is set to one of the following values:

[E2BIG]
The argument *off* in *dm_probe_hole*( ) is larger then file size or the sum of *off* and *len* is beyond the end of the file.

[EACCES]
For *dm_probe_hole*( ), the access right referenced by the token for the handle is not at least DM_RIGHT_SHARED.

[EACCES]
For *dm_punch_hole*( ), the access right referenced by the token for the handle is not DM_RIGHT_EXCL.

[EAGAIN]
Rounding of the offset and length is required for a punch operation.

[EBADF]
The handle does not refer to an existing or accessible object.

[EFAULT]
The system detected an invalid address in attempting to use an argument.

[EINVAL]
The argument *token* is not a valid token.

[EINVAL]
The file handle does not refer to a regular file.

[EINVAL]
The session is not valid.

[EIO]
I/O error resulted in failure of operation.

[ENOSYS]
The DMAPI implementation does not support this optional function.

[EPERM]
The caller does not hold the appropriate privilege.

[EROFS]
The operation is not allowed on a read-only file system.

SEE ALSO

dm_get_allocinfo ( ).

NOTES

The *dm_punch_hole*( ) and *dm_probe_hole*( ) functions are an optional component of the DMAPI.

NAME

dm_query_right — determine the set of access rights to an object

SYNOPSIS

```
int
dm_query_right(
    dm_sessid_t     sid,
    void           *hanp,
    size_t          hlen,
    dm_token_t      token,
    dm_right_t     *rightp)
```

DESCRIPTION

The *dm_query_right*( ) function determines the access rights to the specified object referenced by the token.

dm_sessid_t *sid* (I)
: The identifier for the session of interest.

void **hanp* (I)
: The handle that is being queried for access rights.

size_t *hlen* (I)
: The length of the handle in bytes.

dm_token_t *token* (I)
: The token that references the access rights.

dm_right_t **rightp* (O)
: The location where the access rights should be returned.

RETURN VALUE

Zero is returned on success. On error, -1 is returned, and the global *errno* is set to one of the following values:

[EBADF]
: The file handle does not refer to an existing or accessible object.

[EFAULT]
: The system detected an invalid address in attempting to use an argument.

[EINVAL]
: The session or token is not valid.

[ENOENT]
: The token does not reference any access rights for the handle.

[ENOMEM]
: The DMAPI could not obtain the required resources to complete the call.

[EPERM]
: The caller does not hold the appropriate privilege.

SEE ALSO

dm_create_userevent( ), *dm_request_right*( ), *dm_respond_event*( ).

dm_query_session( )

NAME

dm_query_session — query a session for information

SYNOPSIS

```
int
dm_query_session(
    dm_sessid_t     sid,
    size_t          buflen,
    void           *bufp,
    size_t         *rlenp)
```

DESCRIPTION

DM applications can associate up to DM_SESSION_INFO_LEN bytes of information with a session via the *dm_create_session*( ) function. To retrieve this information during recovery, a DM application must use *dm_query_session*( ).

dm_sessid_t *sid* (I)
: The identifier for the session of interest.

size_t *buflen* (I)
: The length of the input buffer in bytes.

void **bufp* (O)
: The buffer to be filled in with the session information.

size_t **rlenp* (O)
: The size of the requested information. If the buffer is not large enough to hold the requested information (as indicated by the *buflen* parameter), then no data is copied, the call fails with [E2BIG], and *rlenp* is set to the required size. *rlenp* is updated if either the call was successful or the call fails with [E2BIG], but is undefined otherwise.

RETURN VALUE

Zero is returned on success. On error, -1 is returned, and the global *errno* is set to one of the following values:

[E2BIG]
: The information is too large to fit into the buffer.

[EFAULT]
: The system detected an invalid address in attempting to use an argument.

[EINVAL]
: The session is not valid.

[ENOMEM]
: The DMAPI could not obtain the required resources to complete the call.

[EPERM]
: The caller does not hold the appropriate privilege.

SEE ALSO

dm_getall_sessions( ).

NAME

dm_read_invis — reads a file bypassing DMAPI events
dm_write_invis — writes to a file bypassing DMAPI events

SYNOPSIS

```
dm_ssize_t
dm_read_invis(
    dm_sessid_t     sid,
    void           *hanp,
    size_t          hlen,
    dm_token_t      token,
    dm_off_t        off,
    dm_size_t       len,
    void           *bufp)

dm_ssize_t
dm_write_invis(
    dm_sessid_t     sid,
    void           *hanp,
    size_t          hlen,
    dm_token_t      token,
    int             flags,
    dm_off_t        off,
    dm_size_t       len,
    void           *bufp)
```

DESCRIPTION

The *dm_read_invis*( ) and *dm_write_invis*( ) functions read and write files respectively bypassing normal DMAPI event processing. Neither function updates a file's access or modified time stamps. The semantics of the function are the same as in *read*( ) or *write*( ) functions. *Writes* are either synchronous or asynchronous depending on the value of flags. The default is asynchronous. If DM_WRITE_SYNC is specified in flags, the *dm_write_invis*( ) function has the same semantics as a standard *write* followed by an *fsync*(2) call.

dm_sessid_t *sid* (I)
The identifier for the session of interest.

void **hanp* (I)
File handle for the regular file that is read to or written from.

size_t *hlen* (I)
The length of the handle in bytes.

dm_token_t *token* (I)
The token referencing the access right for the file. The access right must be DM_RIGHT_EXCL on writes, and at least DM_RIGHT_SHARED on reads or the token DM_NO_TOKEN may be used and the interface acquires the appropriate rights.

int *flags* (I)
Flags modifying the behavior of *dm_write_invis*( ). Currently the only flag defined is DM_WRITE_SYNC, which causes a write to be synchronous.

dm_off_t *off* (I)
The starting offset in the file to begin reading or writing.

dm_size_t *len* (I)
The length to read or write.

void **bufp* (I/O)
: When reading, this is an output parameter, and is filled in with the data from the file. When writing, it is an input parameter, and contains the data that is written to the file.

RETURN VALUE

Number of bytes read or written on success, -1 on failure and global *errno* is set to one of the following or other implementation specific values:

[EACCES]
: For *dm_read_invis*( ), the access right referenced by the token for the handle is not at least DM_RIGHT_SHARED.

[EACCES]
: For *dm_write_invis*( ), the access right referenced by the token for the handle is not DM_RIGHT_EXCL.

[EBADF]
: The file handle does not refer to an existing or accessible object.

[EFAULT]
: The system detected an invalid address in attempting to use an argument.

[EFBIG]
: For *dm_write_invis*( ), the sum of *off* and *len* is larger than the maximum file size.

[EINTR]
: The operation was interrupted by a signal and should be re-tried. On *dm_write_invis*( ), no data was written to the file.

[EINVAL]
: The argument *len* is too large and will overflow if placed into a **dm_ssize_t** value.

[EINVAL]
: The argument *off* is larger than the file size for read.

[EINVAL]
: The argument *token* is not a valid token.

[EINVAL]
: The file handle does not refer to a regular file.

[EINVAL]
: The session is not valid.

[EIO]
: I/O error resulted in failure of operation.

[ENOSPC]
: No space left in the file system.

[EPERM]
: The caller does not hold the appropriate privilege.

[EROFS]
: The operation is not allowed on a read-only file system.

NAME

dm_release_right — release all access rights to an object

SYNOPSIS

```
int
dm_release_right(
    dm_sessid_t    sid,
    void          *hanp,
    size_t         hlen,
    dm_token_t     token)
```

DESCRIPTION

The access rights referenced by the token for the specified object are released. If the access rights cannot be immediately relinquished, [EAGAIN] is returned.

dm_sessid_t *sid* (I)
: The identifier for the session of interest.

void **hanp* (I)
: The handle for the file system object for which the access rights are being released.

size_t *hlen* (I)
: The length of the handle in bytes.

dm_token_t *token* (I)
: The token referencing the access rights for the specified object.

RETURN VALUE

Zero is returned on success. On error, -1 is returned, and the global *errno* is set to one of the following values:

[EACCES]
: The token does not have rights to the object.

[EAGAIN]
: The right could not be immediately released.

[EBADF]
: The file handle does not refer to an existing or accessible object.

[EBUSY]
: The DMAPI implementation does not support releasing this type of right.

[EFAULT]
: The system detected an invalid address in attempting to use an argument.

[EINVAL]
: The session is not valid.

[EINVAL]
: The token is not valid.

[ENOMEM]
: The DMAPI could not obtain the required resources to complete the call.

[EPERM]
: The caller does not hold the appropriate privilege.

SEE ALSO

dm_request_right( ), *dm_query_right*( ), *dm_create_userevent*( ).

NAME

dm_remove_dmattr — remove a data management attribute

SYNOPSIS

```
int
dm_remove_dmattr(
    dm_sessid_t      sid,
    void            *hanp,
    size_t           hlen,
    dm_token_t       token,
    int              setdtime,
    dm_attrname_t   *attrnamep)
```

DESCRIPTION

The *dm_remove_dmattr*( ) function removes the attribute specified by attrname. When a file is removed, the associated attributes are also removed automatically.

dm_sessid_t *sid* (I)
: The identifier for the session of interest.

void **hanp* (I)
: The handle for the file for which the attributes should be removed.

size_t *hlen* (I)
: The length of the handle in bytes.

dm_token_t *token* (I)
: The token referencing the access right for the handle. The access right must be DM_RIGHT_EXCL or the token DM_NO_TOKEN may be used and the interface acquires the appropriate rights.

int *setdtime* (I)
: The file's attribute time stamp is updated if *setdtime* is non-zero.

dm_attrname_t **attrnamep* (I)
: The attribute to be removed.

RETURN VALUE

Zero is returned on success. On error, -1 is returned, and the global *errno* is set to one of the following values:

[EACCES]
: The access right referenced by the token for the handle is not DM_RIGHT_EXCL.

[EBADF]
: The file handle does not refer to an existing or accessible object.

[EFAULT]
: The system detected an invalid address in attempting to use an argument.

[EINVAL]
: The argument *token* is not a valid token.

[EINVAL]
: The session is not valid.

[EIO]
: I/O error resulted in failure of operation.

[ENOSYS]
The DMAPI implementation does not support this optional function.

[EPERM]
The caller does not hold the appropriate privilege.

[EROFS]
The operation is not allowed on a read-only file system.

SEE ALSO

dm_set_dmattr( ).

NOTES

dm_remove_dmattr( ) is an optional component of the DMAPI.

dm_request_right( )

NAME

dm_request_right — request a specific access right to an object

SYNOPSIS

```
int
dm_request_right(
    dm_sessid_t     sid,
    void           *hanp,
    size_t          hlen,
    dm_token_t      token,
    u_int           flags,
    dm_right_t      right)
```

DESCRIPTION

Add the requested right to the access rights referenced by the token for the object specified by the handle. This is the mechanism by which DM applications can gain specific access rights to an object.

There are two access rights that can be requested: DM_RIGHT_SHARED and DM_RIGHT_EXCL. The *dm_request_right*( ) function does not block and fails with [EAGAIN] when the requested right cannot be obtained. If a DM application needs to block interruptibly until the requested right is available, then the DM_RR_WAIT flag should be set in the flags argument.

If a process holds a shared access right (DM_RIGHT_SHARED) to an object and requests an exclusive right (DM_RIGHT_EXCL) in a non-blocking mode (the DM_RR_WAIT flag is not set in the *flags* argument), then the request fails immediately with [EACCES] and the shared lock is not released.

If a process attempts to upgrade from a DM_RIGHT_SHARED to an DM_RIGHT_EXCL lock in a non-blocking mode (the DM_RR_WAIT flag is not set in the *flags* argument), then the request may work. If the request fails, [EBUSY] is returned, but the shared lock is not released. If the request succeeds, the shared lock may have been released before the exclusive lock was obtained.

When requesting access rights to an object via *dm_request_right*( ), the requested right may not be immediately available. If the DM application has specified that it wants to block until the right becomes available, the DM application may or may not be blocked interruptibly. The implementation of the DMAPI specifes the semantics that apply for interrupting blocked processes. When interrupts are allowed and occur, the call fails with [EINTR].

dm_sessid_t *sid* (I)
: The identifier for the session of interest.

void **hanp* (I)
: The handle for the file system object for which access rights are being requested.

size_t *hlen* (I)
: The length of the handle in bytes.

dm_token_t *token* (I)
: The token that references the access rights for the object to be manipulated. DM_NO_TOKEN cannot be used with *dm_request_right*( ).

u_int *flags* (I)
: If the DM_RR_WAIT flag is not set and the requested right is not available, the calling process fails with [EAGAIN]. If DM_RR_WAIT is set and the requested right is not available, the calling process blocks interruptibly, waiting for the requested right to become

available.

dm_right_t *right* (I)
The requested access right.

USAGE NOTES

See Section 2.5 on page 10 for more information about how *dm_request_right*( ) should be used.

RETURN VALUE

Zero is returned on success. On error, -1 is returned, and the global *errno* is set to one of the following values:

[EACCES]
The process attempted to upgrade a lock in blocking mode.

[EAGAIN]
The *flags* parameter did not have the DM_RR_WAIT flag set, and the process would be blocked in requesting the right.

[EBADF]
The file handle does not refer to an existing or accessible object.

[EBUSY]
The upgrade from DM_RIGHT_SHARED to DM_RIGHT_EXCL cannot be granted.

[EFAULT]
The system detected an invalid address in attempting to use an argument.

[EINTR]
The DMAPI implementation allows interruption and the process was interrupted.

[EINVAL]
The requested right is not valid.

[EINVAL]
The session or token is not valid or token was DM_NO_TOKEN.

[ENOMEM]
The DMAPI could not obtain the required resources to complete the call.

[EPERM]
The caller does not hold the appropriate privilege.

SEE ALSO

dm_create_userevent( ), *dm_respond_event*( ), *dm_release_right*( ), *dm_get_fileattr*( ), *dm_query_right*( ).

NAME

dm_respond_event — respond to an event

SYNOPSIS

```
int
dm_respond_event(
    dm_sessid_t      sid,
    dm_token_t       token,
    dm_response_t    response,
    int              reterror,
    size_t           buflen,
    void            *respbufp)
```

DESCRIPTION

Once a synchronous message has been received via *dm_get_events*( ), it must be responded to. Otherwise, the application that caused the event to be generated is blocked, system resources is tied up, and so forth.

The token identifies the message. Once this call has returned, the token is no longer valid.

Some DMAPI implementations may provide extensions to the basic event facility, such as the ability to return attribute information when responding to an event. These extensions will utilize the *respbufp* parameter. Normal event responses will only make use of the response code and corresponding *reterror* value.

dm_sessid_t *sid* (I)
The identifier for the session of interest.

dm_token_t *token* (I)
The token identifying the message.

dm_response_t *response* (I)
The action to be taken by the operating system. Valid actions are DM_RESP_CONTINUE, which continues the operation, or DM_RESP_ABORT, which aborts the operation and sets the *errno* of the calling process to *reterror*. DM_RESP_DONTCARE is also valid when responding to the *mount* event.

int *reterror* (I)
If the operation is to be aborted (response is set to DM_RESP_ABORT), return *errno* to the application that caused the event. *reterror* is returned to the user, even if it is set to zero.

size_t *buflen* (I)
The length of the response buffer in bytes. Only used by implementations that provide extensions to the DMAPI.

void **respbufp* (I)
Buffer for DMAPI implementation extensions. The format of this buffer is not defined by the DMAPI.

RETURN VALUE

Zero is returned on success. On error, -1 is returned, and the global *errno* is set to one of the following values:

[E2BIG]
buflen is larger than the implementation defined limit. The limit can be determined by calling the *dm_get_config*( ) function using DM_CONFIG_MAX_ATTRIBUTE_SIZE.

[EFAULT]
The system detected an invalid address in attempting to use an argument.

[EINVAL]
The session is not valid.

[ENOMEM]
The DMAPI could not obtain the required resources to complete the call.

[EPERM]
The caller does not hold the appropriate privilege.

[ESRCH]
The token does not reference a valid message.

SEE ALSO

dm_get_events( ).

NAME

dm_send_msg — send a message to the indicated session

SYNOPSIS

```
int
dm_send_msg(
    dm_sessid_t      targetsid,
    dm_msgtype_t     msgtype,
    size_t           buflen,
    void            *bufp)
```

DESCRIPTION

The *dm_send_msg*( ) function allows an event message of type user to be enqueued on the indicated session. The contents of the message data are opaque to the DMAPI. The message remains enqueued until the indicated target session receives it with *dm_get_events*( ).

dm_send_msg( ) can send both synchronous and asynchronous messages. If the type is DM_MSGTYPE_SYNC, then a synchronous message is created, and the calling process blocks until a response is returned. The DMAPI generates a token that references no access rights. If the type is DM_MSGTYPE_ASYNC, then an asynchronous event message is created, and the calling process is not blocked. The DMAPI does not generate a token for asynchronous messages. The lack of a valid token is identified to the receiver of the event by a value of DM_INVALID_TOKEN in the token field of the event message.

dm_sessid_t *targetsid* (I)
: The session the message should be enqueued upon.

dm_msgtype_t *msgtype* (I)
: The type of message to be enqueued: DM_MSGTYPE_SYNC or DM_MSGTYPE_ASYNC.

size_t *buflen* (I)
: The length of the data buffer in bytes.

void **bufp* (I)
: The data that is to be incorporated into the generated message. If *buflen* is zero, this parameter is ignored.

RETURN VALUE

Upon successful completion, the function *dm_send_msg*( ) returns zero for asynchronous messages. The return value for synchronous messages is dependent on the return code from the event servicing. Otherwise a value of -1 is returned and *errno* is set to one of the following values:

[E2BIG]
: The user message data is too big to fit into implementation defined limit. The limit can be determined by calling the *dm_get_config*( ) function using DM_CONFIG_MAX_MESSAGE_DATA.

[EFAULT]
: The system detected an invalid address in attempting to use an argument.

[EINTR]
: Interrupted. The event was not delivered.

[EINVAL]
: The session is not valid.

[EINVAL]
: The type is not DM_MSGTYPE_SYNC or DM_MSGTYPE_ASYNC.

[ENOMEM]
The DMAPI could not obtain the required resources to complete the call.

[EPERM]
The caller does not hold the appropriate privilege.

SEE ALSO

dm_get_events( ), *dm_create_userevent*( ).

dm_set_disp( )

NAME

dm_set_disp — set the disposition of events on a file system for a session

SYNOPSIS

```
int
dm_set_disp(
    dm_sessid_t     sid,
    void           *hanp,
    size_t          hlen,
    dm_token_t      token,
    dm_eventset_t  *eventsetp,
    u_int           maxevent)
```

DESCRIPTION

After establishing a session, a DM application must indicate which events to deliver to the session. The event set is the complete set of all events, including managed region events, that the DM application is monitoring during the life of this session. This event set is not persistent across reboots.

The *dm_set_disp*( ) function establishes a (event, file system, session) binding that lets the DMAPI implementation know which session to send events to. Until it has completed, the DMAPI implementation has no way of knowing what session should receive events that are generated on a file system. Once *dm_set_disp*( ) has returned to the calling DM application, the session starts receiving events as they are generated by the DMAPI implementation.

If a specific event in *eventsetp* already has been established for the file system indicated by *hanp*, then the prior (event, file system, session) binding is replaced by the one specified by the *eventsetp* parameter. It is not possible to target the same event to multiple sessions simultaneously (except for the special case of the *mount* event).

DM applications must register the event list and session binding using a file system handle; it is not possible to use arbitrary file system objects (such as regular files). Since the file system handle can only be obtained after the file system has been mounted, it is not possible to specify the *mount* event using the file system handle. The global handle must be used. If the *mount* event is specified using the file system handle, the behavior is undefined. If events other than the *mount* event are specified for the global handle, the behavior is also undefined.

dm_sessid_t *sid* (I)
: The identifier for the session of interest.

void **hanp* (I)
: The handle for the file system or the global handle.

size_t *hlen* (I)
: The length of the handle in bytes.

dm_token_t *token* (I)
: The token referencing the access right for the handle. The access right must be DM_RIGHT_EXCL or the token DM_NO_TOKEN may be used and the interface acquires the appropriate rights.

dm_eventset_t **eventsetp* (I)
: The list of default events to be monitored for this session.

u_int *maxevent* (I)
: The number of events to be checked for dispositions in the event set. The events from 0 to *maxevent–1* are examined.

RETURN VALUE

Zero is returned on success. On error, -1 is returned, and the global *errno* is set to one of the following values:

[EACCES]
The access right referenced by the token for the handle is not DM_RIGHT_EXCL.

[EBADF]
The file handle does not refer to an existing or accessible object.

[EFAULT]
The system detected an invalid address in attempting to use an argument.

[EINVAL]
The handle is not a file system handle.

[EINVAL]
The session is not valid.

[EINVAL]
The token is not valid.

[ENOMEM]
The DMAPI could not obtain the required resources to complete the call.

[ENXIO]
The implementation of the DMAPI does not support registering for events on the specified handle.

[EPERM]
The caller does not hold the appropriate privilege.

SEE ALSO

dm_create_session( ), *dm_set_eventlist*( ), *dm_getall_disp*( ).

dm_set_dmattr( )

NAME

dm_set_dmattr — create or replace a data management attribute

SYNOPSIS

```
int
dm_set_dmattr(
    dm_sessid_t      sid,
    void            *hanp,
    size_t           hlen,
    dm_token_t       token,
    dm_attrname_t   *attrnamep,
    int              setdtime,
    size_t           buflen,
    void            *bufp)
```

DESCRIPTION

The *dm_set_dmattr*( ) function creates or replaces the value of the named attribute with the specified data.

dm_sessid_t *sid* (I)
The identifier for the session of interest.

void **hanp* (I)
The handle for the file for which the attributes should be created or replaced.

size_t *hlen* (I)
The length of the handle in bytes.

dm_token_t *token* (I)
The token referencing the access right for the handle. The access right must be DM_RIGHT_EXCL or the token DM_NO_TOKEN may be used and the interface acquires the appropriate rights.

dm_attrname_t **attrnamep* (I)
The attribute to be created or replaced.

int *setdtime* (I)
The file's attribute time stamp is updated if *setdtime* is non-zero.

size_t *buflen* (I)
The size of the buffer in bytes.

void **bufp* (I)
The buffer containing the attribute data.

RETURN VALUE

Zero is returned on success. On error, -1 is returned, and the global *errno* is set to one of the following values:

[E2BIG]
The attribute value exceeds one of the implementation definied storage limits.

[E2BIG]
buflen is larger than the implementation defined limit. The limit can be determined by calling the *dm_get_config*( ) function.

[EACCES]
The access right referenced by the token for the handle is not DM_RIGHT_EXCL.

[EBADF]
The file handle does not refer to an existing or accessible object.

[EFAULT]
The system detected an invalid address in attempting to use an argument.

[EIO]
An attempt to write the new or updated attribute resulted in an I/O error.

[EINVAL]
The argument *token* is not a valid token.

[EINVAL]
The session is not valid.

[ENOMEM]
The DMAPI could not acquire the required resources to complete the call.

[ENOSPC]
An attempt to write the new or updated attribute resulted in an error due to no free space being available on the device.

[ENOSYS]
The DMAPI implementation does not support this optional function.

[EPERM]
The caller does not hold the appropriate privilege.

[EROFS]
The operation is not allowed on a read-only file system.

SEE ALSO

dm_get_dmattr( ), *dm_remove_dmattr*( ), *dm_getall_dmattr*( ).

NOTES

dm_set_dmattr( ) is an optional component of the DMAPI.

NAME

dm_set_eventlist — set the list of events to be enabled for an object

SYNOPSIS

```
int
dm_set_eventlist(
    dm_sessid_t       sid,
    void             *hanp,
    size_t            hlen,
    dm_token_t        token,
    dm_eventset_t    *eventsetp,
    u_int             maxevent)
```

DESCRIPTION

To receive events on an object, a DM application must bind a set of events to an object, indicating to the DMAPI that the application is monitoring the object. The *dm_set_eventlist*( ) function establishes a binding of events on the indicated object that may be persistent. Persistence of event bindings is implementation defined, and can be determined via the *dm_get_config*( ) function.

The two functions *dm_set_disp*( ) and *dm_set_eventlist*( ) work together to enable DM applications to receive events. *dm_set_eventlist*( ) controls the generation of events on an object, by specifying which file system operations should generate a DMAPI event. *dm_set_disp*( ) controls the delivery of events by specifying which session should receive the generated event.

Events can be enabled on any file system object, including regular files. The managed region events cannot be specified via *dm_set_eventlist*( ) since they are specific to each managed region. The *mount* event cannot be specified, since it is generated by all file system types that support the DMAPI.

dm_sessid_t *sid* (I)
    The identifier for the session of interest.

void **hanp* (I)
    The handle for the object. The handle can be either the file system handle or a file handle.

size_t *hlen* (I)
    The length of the handle in bytes.

dm_token_t *token* (I)
    The token referencing the access right for the handle. The access right must be DM_RIGHT_EXCL or the token DM_NO_TOKEN may be used and the interface acquires the appropriate rights.

dm_eventset_t **eventsetp* (I)
    The list of events to be enabled for the object.

u_int *maxevent* (I)
    The number of events to be checked for dispositions in the event set. The events from 0 to *maxevent–1* are examined.

RETURN VALUE

Zero is returned on success. On error, -1 is returned, and the global *errno* is set to one of the following values:

[EACCES]
    The access right referenced by the token for the handle is not DM_RIGHT_EXCL.

[EBADF]
The file handle does not refer to an existing or accessible object.

[EFAULT]
The system detected an invalid address in attempting to use an argument.

[EINVAL]
The argument *token* is not a valid token.

[EINVAL]
The session is not valid.

[EINVAL]
Tried to set event on a global handle.

[ENOMEM]
The DMAPI could not obtain the required resources to complete the call.

[ENXIO]
The implementation of the DMAPI does not support enabling event delivery on the specified handle.

[EPERM]
The caller does not hold the appropriate privilege.

[EROFS]
The operation is not allowed on a read-only file system.

SEE ALSO

dm_get_eventlist( ), *dm_set_disp*( ), *dm_set_region*( ), macro DMEV_SET .

NAME

dm_set_fileattr — set file time stamps, ownership and mode

SYNOPSIS

```
int
dm_set_fileattr(
    dm_sessid_t      sid,
    void            *hanp,
    size_t           hlen,
    dm_token_t       token,
    u_int            mask,
    dm_fileattr_t   *attrp)
```

DESCRIPTION

The *dm_set_fileattr*( ) function allows DM applications to set various file attributes as defined by the **dm_fileattr** structure.

Each field corresponding to a bit in the mask is used to set the corresponding attribute in the file. For fields that are not specified to be set, the current value is not modified. For example, if DM_AT_CTIME is not set, the file's *ctime* field is not modified.

If the call to *dm_set_fileattr*( ) requests updates of both *dm_ctime* and *dm_dtime*, and the DMAPI implementation overloads *dm_ctime* and *dm_dtime*, then *dm_ctime* is used.

dm_sessid_t *sid* (I)
: The identifier for the session of interest.

void **hanp* (I)
: The handle for the file for which the file attributes should be set.

size_t *hlen* (I)
: The length of the handle in bytes.

dm_token_t *token* (I)
: The token referencing the access right for the handle. The access right must be DM_RIGHT_EXCL or the token DM_NO_TOKEN may be used and the interface acquires the appropriate rights.

u_int *mask* (I)
: The argument mask indicates which fields of the **dm_fileattr** structure to set. The mask is constructed by OR-ing together one or more of the following flags:

DM_AT_ATIME
: The file's access time stamp.

DM_AT_MTIME
: The file's data modification time stamp.

DM_AT_CTIME
: The file's status change time stamp.

DM_AT_DTIME
: The time stamp of the persistent attributes if associated with the file. The value is ignored if no DM attributes exist.

DM_AT_UID
: User ID of the file's owner.

DM_AT_GID
: Group ID of the file's owner.

DM_AT_MODE
The mode of the file as described by the *mknod*(2) system call.

DM_AT_SIZE
The size of the file. May cause a system dependent error to occur, possibly a ENOSPC.

dm_fileattr_t **attrp* (I)
The **dm_fileattr** structure with the appropriate fields defined. For fields that are not set, the corresponding fields of the **dm_fileattr** structure are not used.

RETURN VALUE

Zero is returned on success. On error, -1 is returned, and the global *errno* is set to one of the following values:

[EACCES]
The access right referenced by the token for the handle is not DM_RIGHT_EXCL.

[EBADF]
The file handle does not refer to an existing or accessible object.

[EFAULT]
The system detected an invalid address in attempting to use an argument.

[EINVAL]
The argument *mask* is not valid.

[EINVAL]
The argument *token* is not a valid token.

[EINVAL]
The session is not valid.

[EIO]
I/O error resulted in failure of operation.

[ENOMEM]
The DMAPI could not acquire the required resources to complete the call.

[EPERM]
The caller does not hold the appropriate privilege.

[EROFS]
The operation is not allowed on a read-only file system.

SEE ALSO

dm_fileattr_t( ).

NAME

dm_set_inherit — mark an attribute inheritable

SYNOPSIS

```
int
dm_set_inherit(
    dm_sessid_t     sid,
    void           *hanp,
    size_t          hlen,
    dm_toke n_t     token,
    dm_attrname_t  *attrnamep,
    mode_t          mode)
```

DESCRIPTION

The function *dm_set_inherit*( ) marks the attribute specified by *attrnamep* as an inheritable attribute for the file system specified by the handle. An attribute is inherited from the parent directory during file creation. The inheritability property of attributes is not persistent across reboots. The access right referenced by the token for the object must be DM_RIGHT_EXCL.

dm_sessid_t *sid* (I)
The identifier for the session of interest.

void **hanp* (I)
The file system handle for which the inheritable attributes should be set.

size_t *hlen* (I)
The length of the handle in bytes.

dm_token_t *token* (I)
The token referencing the access right for the handle. The access right must be DM_RIGHT_EXCL or the token DM_NO_TOKEN may be used and the interface acquires the appropriate rights.

dm_attrname_t **attrnamep* (I)
The attribute to be marked as inheritable.

mode_t *mode* (I)
The argument mode limits the scope of inheritance to file objects created of specified values. *mode* is taken from Single UNIX Specification values.

RETURN VALUE

Zero is returned on success. On error, -1 is returned, and the global *errno* is set to one of the following values:

[EACCES]
The access right referenced by the token for the handle is not DM_RIGHT_EXCL.

[EBADF]
The handle does not refer to an existing or accessible object.

[EFAULT]
The system detected an invalid address in attempting to use an argument.

[EINVAL]
The argument *hanp* does not refer to a file system handle.

[EINVAL]
The argument *mode* does not contain valid file types.

[EINVAL]
The session or token is not valid.

[ENOMEM]
The DMAPI could not acquire the required resources to complete the call.

[ENOSYS]
The DMAPI implementation does not support this optional function.

[EPERM]
The caller does not hold the appropriate privilege.

SEE ALSO

dm_clear_inherit( ), *dm_getall_inherit*( ).

NOTES

dm_set_inherit( ) is an optional component of the DMAPI.

NAME

dm_set_region — set the managed regions for a file

SYNOPSIS

```
int
dm_set_region(
    dm_sessid_t     sid,
    void           *hanp,
    size_t          hlen,
    dm_token_t      token,
    u_int           nelem,
    dm_region_t    *regbufp,
    dm_boolean_t   *exactflagp)
```

DESCRIPTION

The *dm_set_region*( ) function replaces the set of managed regions for a regular file. The implementation has the right to round the boundaries or change the number of managed regions. The final set of managed regions must cover the requested regions. Overlapping managed regions are not permitted.

The **dm_region** structure defines the range of bytes that are managed in the file. The *rg_flags* field can be set to generate synchronous read, write, and truncate events whenever the associated operation is performed within the managed region. A region may extend outside the current valid portions of a file. A region may extend to the end of a file and allow control on files that are appended to, by setting *rg_size* to zero. Regions may also be allocated with no associated events set by using DM_REGION_NOEVENT. This may be used to allocate space for future control of a region of the file in DMAPI implementations that provide persistent managed regions.

The implementation is free to reorder the managed region set. A subsequent call to *dm_get_region*( ) may return the managed regions in a different order than they were provided to *dm_set_region*( ). The DMAPI implementation is also permitted to coalesce contiguous or noncontiguous regions with identical *rg_flags*. The *exactflagp* is set to DM_TRUE if the file system did not alter the managed region set.

For operations involving multiple managed regions within a file, only one region event is generated for the operation. It is up to the DM application to respond appropriately to all managed regions that are affected by an operation.

dm_sessid_t *sid* (I)
: The identifier for the session of interest.

void **hanp* (I)
: Handle for the regular file to be affected.

size_t *hlen* (I)
: The length of the handle in bytes.

dm_token_t *token* (I)
: The token referencing the access right for the handle. The access right must be DM_RIGHT_EXCL or the token DM_NO_TOKEN may be used and the interface acquires the appropriate rights.

u_int *nelem* (I)
: The number of input regions in *regbufp*. If *nelem* is 0, then all existing managed regions are cleared.

dm_region_t **regbufp* (I)
A pointer to the structure defining the regions to be set. May be NULL if *nelem* is zero.

dm_boolean_t **exactflagp* (O)
If DM_TRUE, the file system did not alter the requested managed region set.

Valid values for the *rg_flags* field of the region structure are created by OR'ing together one or more of the following values:

DM_REGION_READ
Enable synchronous event for read operations that overlap this managed region.

DM_REGION_WRITE
Enable synchronous event for write operations that overlap this managed region.

DM_REGION_TRUNCATE
Enable synchronous event for truncate operations that overlap this managed region.

DM_REGION_NOEVENT
Do not generate any events for this managed region.

RETURN VALUE

Zero is returned on success. On error, -1 is returned, and the global *errno* is set to one of the following values:

[E2BIG]
The number of regions specified by *nelem* exceeded the implementation capacity.

[EACCES]
The access right referenced by the token for the handle is not DM_RIGHT_EXCL.

[EBADF]
The file handle does not refer to an existing or accessible object.

[EFAULT]
The system detected an invalid address in attempting to use an argument.

[EINVAL]
The argument *token* is not a valid token.

[EINVAL]
The file handle does not refer to a regular file.

[EINVAL]
The regions passed in are not valid because they overlap or some other problem.

[EINVAL]
The session is not valid.

[EIO]
An I/O error resulted in failure of operation.

[ENOMEM]
The DMAPI could not acquire the required resources to complete the call.

[EPERM]
The caller does not hold the appropriate privilege.

[EROFS]
The operation is not allowed on a read-only file system.

SEE ALSO

dm_get_region( ), *dm_get_eventlist*( ).

NAME

dm_set_return_on_destroy — specify a DM attribute to return with destroy events

SYNOPSIS

```
int
dm_set_return_on_destroy(
    dm_sessid_t       sid,
    void             *hanp,
    size_t            hlen,
    dm_token_t        token,
    dm_attrname_t    *attrnamep,
    dm_boolean_t      enable)
```

DESCRIPTION

The *dm_set_return_on_destroy*( ) function allows a DM application to specify one data management attribute whose data is returned with *destroy* events generated for the specified file system. The implementation, if it supports persistent attributes, delivers a copy of the attribute data with *destroy* events generated after this function returns successfully.

The data may be truncated if it was greater than the maximum number of bytes that the implementation can return (returned by *dm_get_config*( ) for the DM_MAX_ATTR_BYTES_ON_DESTROY flag). If a destroyed object on the file system did not have the specified attribute set, then no data is returned with the corresponding *destroy* events.

This binding does not persist after unmounting of the file system.

dm_sessid_t *sid* (I)
: The identifier for the session of interest.

void **hanp* (I)
: The handle for the file system of interest.

size_t *hlen* (I)
: The length of the handle in bytes.

dm_token_t *token* (I)
: The token referencing the access right for the handle. The access right must be DM_RIGHT_EXCL or the token DM_NO_TOKEN may be used and the interface acquires the appropriate rights.

dm_attrname_t **attrnamep* (I)
: The attribute to be returned with *destroy* events.

dm_boolean_t *enable* (I)
: Set to DM_TRUE to enable returning attributes. Set to DM_FALSE to disable returning attributes.

Return Values

Zero is returned on success. On error, -1 is returned, and the global *errno* is set to one of the following values:

[EACCES]
: The access right referenced by the token for the handle is not DM_RIGHT_EXCL.

[EBADF]
: The handle does not refer to an existing or accessible object.

[EFAULT]
: The system detected an invalid address in attempting to use an argument.

[EINVAL]
The argument *token* is not a valid token.

[EINVAL]
The handle does not refer to a file system.

[EINVAL]
The session is not valid.

[EINVAL]
The attribute name is not valid.

[ENOSYS]
The DMAPI implementation does not support this optional function.

[EPERM]
The caller does not hold the appropriate privilege.

SEE ALSO

dm_set_eventlist( ).

NOTES

dm_set_return_on_destroy( ) is an optional component of the DMAPI.

NAME

dm_symlink_by_handle — create a symbolic link using a DM handle

SYNOPSIS

```
int
dm_symlink_by_handle(
    dm_sessid_t    sid,
    void          *dirhanp,
    size_t         dirhlen,
    dm_token_t     token,
    void          *hanp,
    size_t         hlen,
    char          *cname,
    char          *path)
```

DESCRIPTION

The *dm_symlink_by_handle*( ) function allows applications the ability to create a symbolic link in a directory specified by *dirhanp* and with a component name specified by *cname* that can, after creation, be referenced by the supplied target handle hanp. This is useful when an application is reconstructing a file system object for which it still has the data and attributes stored on alternate media.

This function creates the link with the specified path as its value (that is, the new object created will be a symbolic link pointing to path)

It is the responsibility of the user of this function to reconstruct the object state including extended attributes. See *dm_set_fileattr*( ) and *dm_set_dmattr*( ).

If an object cannot be constructed by the file system for the specified handle, an error is returned.

dm_sessid_t *sid* (I)
: The identifier for the session of interest.

void **dirhanp* (I)
: The handle for the directory that contains the target file.

size_t *dirhlen* (I)
: The length of the directory handle in bytes.

dm_token_t *token* (I)
: The token referencing the access right for the directory handle. The access right must be at DM_RIGHT_EXCL or the token DM_NO_TOKEN may be used and the interface acquires the appropriate rights.

void **hanp* (I)
: The file handle of the symbolic link.

size_t *hlen* (I)
: The length of the file handle in bytes.

char **cname* (I)
: The name of the symbolic link to be created in the specified directory.

char **path* (I)
: The path to which the symbolic link points.

RETURN VALUE

Zero is returned on success. On error, -1 is returned, and the global *errno* is set to one of the following values:

[EACCES]
The access right referenced by the token for the directory handle is not DM_RIGHT_EXCL.

[EBADF]
The parent directory handle does not refer to an existing or accessible object.

[EEXIST]
The file handle refers to an existing object.

[EFAULT]
The system detected an invalid address in attempting to use an argument.

[EINVAL]
The argument *token* is not a valid token.

[EINVAL]
The session is not valid.

[ENOSYS]
The DMAPI implementation does not support this optional function.

[EPERM]
The caller does not hold the appropriate privilege.

SEE ALSO

dm_set_fileattr( ), *dm_set_dmattr*( ), *dm_create_by_handle*( ), *dm_mkdir_by_handle*( ).

NOTES

dm_symlink_by_handle( ) is an optional component of the DMAPI.

NAME

dm_sync_by_handle — synchronize a file's in-memory state with that on the physical medium

SYNOPSIS

```
int
dm_sync_by_handle(
    dm_sessid_t    sid,
    void          *hanp,
    size_t         hlen,
    dm_token_t     token)
```

DESCRIPTION

The *dm_sync_by_handle*( ) function causes all modified data and attributes of the object referred to by *hanp* to be written to its physical media. When *dm_sync_by_handle*( ) returns, the state of the object referred to by *hanp* is captured on physical medium. This is the equivalent of *fsync*(2), except that the object is referenced by the handle.

dm_sessid_t *sid* (I)
The identifier for the session of interest.

void **hanp* (I)
A handle to any file in the file system.

size_t *hlen* (I)
The length of the handle in bytes.

dm_token_t *token* (I)
The token referencing the access right for the handle. The access right must be at DM_RIGHT_EXCL or the token DM_NO_TOKEN may be used and the interface acquires the appropriate rights.

RETURN VALUE

Zero is returned on success. On error, -1 is returned, and the global *errno* is set to one of the following values:

[EACCES]
The access right referenced by the token for the handle is not DM_RIGHT_EXCL.

[EBADF]
hanp does not refer to an existing or accessible object.

[EFAULT]
The system detected an invalid address in attempting to use an argument.

[EINVAL]
The argument *token* is not a valid token.

[ENOMEM]
The DMAPI could not obtain the required resources to complete the call.

[ENOSYS]
The DMAPI implementation does not support this optional function.

[EPERM]
The caller does not hold the appropriate privilege.

NOTES

dm_sync_by_handle( ) is an optional component of the DMAPI.

dm_upgrade_right( )

NAME

dm_upgrade_right — upgrade a currently held access right to an exclusive right

SYNOPSIS

```
int
dm_upgrade_right(
    dm_sessid_t     sid,
    void           *hanp,
    size_t          hlen,
    dm_token_t      token)
```

DESCRIPTION

Upgrade the access right currently held for the object specified by the handle and referenced by the token. The upgrade operation does not drop the access right currently held for the object and attempts to upgrade without blocking the process requesting to upgrade.

The minimum *right* to hold when making this request is DM_RIGHT_SHARED. If a process requests to upgrade while holding an exclusive *right*, the request succeeds with no attempt to upgrade. Otherwise the attempt to upgrade is tried without blocking the process. If the requested *right* cannot be obtained without blocking, the request fails.

On DMAPI implementations that do not support non-blocking *right* upgrades, this call fails with [ENOSYS].

dm_sessid_t *sid* (I)
: The identifier for the session of interest.

void **hanp* (I)
: The handle for the file system object for which upgrading access right is being requested and with which an access right is already associated. See also *dm_downgrade_right*( ) on page 80.

size_t *hlen* (I)
: The length of the handle in bytes.

dm_token_t *token* (I)
: The token referencing the access right for the object.

IMPLEMENTATION NOTE

A DM application may retry upgrading an access right if *dm_upgrade_right*( ) fails with [EBUSY]. This is an indication that there is at least one other process holding a shared access right to the same object. Note that the request to upgrade can only be granted if the requesting process is the only holder of a shared or exclusive right to the object. In the case of another process holding a shared right to the same object, the requesting process must be aware of possible deadlock that can be caused when at least one other process tries to upgrade its access right.

RETURN VALUE

Zero is returned on success. On error, -1 is returned, and the global *errno* is set to one of the following values:

[EBADF]
: The file handle does not refer to an existing or accessible object.

[EBUSY]
: Could not upgrade access right.

[EFAULT]
: The system detected an invalid address in attempting to use an argument.

[EINVAL]
The token does not grant a DM_RIGHT_SHARED or DM_RIGHT_EXCL to the specified object.

[ENOSYS]
The DMAPI implementation does not support this optional function.

[ESRCH]
The token does not refer to any outstanding DM event.

[EPERM]
The caller does not hold the appropriate privilege.

[EPERM]
The access right currently held is not DM_RIGHT_SHARED nor DM_RIGHT_EXCL.

SEE ALSO

dm_downgrade_right ( ), *dm_release_right(),* ( ) *dm_request_right* ( ).

NOTES

dm_upgrade_right ( ) is an optional component of the DMAPI.

Chapter 6

Implementation Notes

This Chapter describes some issues and hints which may be of use to the implementer of the DMAPI. These hints are presented in a separate Chapter because they are relevant to the DMAPI, yet they may not be applicable to all DMAPI implementations.

6.1 Event Encoding

As discussed in the Non-opaque Data Management Attributes section (see Section 2.10.1 on page 17), event bit masks may exist that allow specific encoding of events to be represented with a number of fixed bit patterns. These bit patterns are implementation defined, are not guaranteed to be the same from platform to platform, and in fact are not visible through any of the DMAPI interfaces.

A single bit might allow the following event list encoding:

0 The file has no event lists.

1 The file has an event list but there is not enough persistent storage available to encode the events.

By increasing the number of bits, well known combinations of events can be stored persistently with the file. For example, with 2 bits, the following event list encoding may exist:

00 The file has no event lists.

01 Read events will be generated for this file.

10 Write events will be generated for this file.

11 The file has an event list but there is not enough persistent storage available to encode the events.

For example, if the file has both read and write events set, then this cannot be encoded in two bits. In this case the *debut* event would need to be generated in order to load the event list.

The encoding of events is not defined by the DMAPI. It is expected that different DMAPI implementations would encode events differently, depending on those data management applications which would be supported.

Note: Due to the requirement regarding implementation of the DMAPI, support for persistent non-opaque attributes is a DMAPI implementation option.

6.2 Event Ordering

Each implementation of the DMAPI may send a number of different events to a DM application as a result of a single system call. It may be helpful, but is not required, for DM application writers to know in advance the sequence of events for each system call. Unfortunately, determining this list is a non-trivial exercise. It is suggested that the DM application writer should work with the implementor of the DMAPI in order to determine the sequence and ordering of events that occurs for system calls of interest.

If the application is multi-threaded, then the DM app writer's job is even more difficult. Synchronization primitives are necessary so that one process is not left hanging waiting for an event that has been serviced by another process.

6.3 Lock Releasing

Some DMAPI implementations may have special lock restrictions. Some may be unable to upgrade an access right from DM_RIGHT_SHARED to DM_RIGHT_EXCL without sleeping, while others may have special primitives that allow them to grant whatever right the DM application requires. Some DMAPI implementations may also have special requirements with regard to releasing locks. During the servicing of events, it may not always be possible to relinquish a right. DM application writers should not assume that it is always possible to release a *right* (via *dm_release_right*()). The careful DM application writer will always check return codes from all DMAPI functions.

6.4 Tokens, Messages and Handles

Tokens reference access rights for handles, and must always be associated with a message. An implementor may wish to view a token as simply a message ID. When viewed this way, the token is similar to a file descriptor, in that it just references state maintained in the kernel. Given the one-to-one correspondence of tokens and messages, one can think of them (within the kernel) as separate objects or one object independent of how they are actually implemented.

6.5 mmap

There are many operating systems that use *mmap*(2) as a mechanism for utilities to copy file data. Unfortunately, this can make implementation of the DMAPI difficult, since a page fault often occurs at a much later point in time than when the file is actually mapped. Usually, there are also very stringent locking restrictions in place at the time the page fault occurs.

To get around these problems, some systems may have to adopt a paradigm that at the time the file is mapped (that is, at the time the actual *mmap*(2) call is executed), then if the file is non-resident it will have to be made resident. This is sub-optimal from a disk space utilization standpoint, and it also means that a large file that is *mmap'd* cannot be partially resident. However, the alternative is to place DMAPI call-outs deep in the VM subsystem, which is usually a very complex exercise and is not recommended unless considerable expertise is available.

6.6 Invisible I/O

Invisible read and write can also place special burdens on the implementor of the DMAPI. Invisible I/O is typically used by a DM application to reload data for a non-resident file. This operation should not modify any of a file's time stamps, nor should it cause events to be generated.

In systems where pages are encached on the vnode, this can lead to troublesome locking and coherency issues. How is the actual write to disk performed? Is the page cache bypassed? How do you ensure that encached pages are dealt with correctly?

6.7 Generation of Events

The placement of code that actually generates events will be different from platform to platform. When an event is actually generated will be different on all systems, and should not concern the DM application writer. The DMAPI implementor will need to take into consideration lock state, likelihood of the operation succeeding, and so forth, to determine the best location for the actual callout to occur.

In the case of managed region events, the DMAPI implementor must ensure that a poorly-behaved DM application does not cause the system to behave in an unexpected manner. For example, if a file has multiple managed regions that represent non-resident data, and a DM application only restores the data for one of those regions, the system must be sure that operations such as *read-ahead* do not cause multiple events to occur. For further information, see the Managed Region description in Section 1.3 on page 2.

6.8 Locking Across Operations

To ensure consistency, some DM application may wish to enforce their own locking scheme across operations. They may want to develop a wrapper around some operations in order to synchronize and/or serialize accesses to files.

6.9 Tokens and Multiple Handles

Tokens may reference access rights for more than one file handle. This makes certain operations easier, such as obtaining access rights to a list of file handles; the same token can be reused without incurring the overhead of *dm_create_userevent*( ) to construct a new token for each file handle. However, allowing a single token to reference multiple handles can make recovery more difficult. How does a DM application determine which file handles have access rights referenced by a single token?

During recovery, a DM application can always execute *dm_respond_event*( ), give it the offending token, and let the DMAPI release any and all access rights associated with the token. If the DM application needs to be selective about which file handles have their access rights released, then it (the DM application) must provide some mechanism external to the DMAPI to log which file handles are associated with a token. The DMAPI does not provide interfaces to identify multiple file handles from a single token.

6.10 Structure Lists

Several DMAPI functions return lists of structures. Some of these functions return lists of variable-length structures. Since the length of the structure is not known, DMAPI implementations must provide a mechanism for the DM application to access the various members of the list.

The DMAPI specifies that DM applications should use the DM_STEP_TO_NEXT macro to access variable length structures that are in a list. However, the actual implementation of this macro is not defined. One suggestion is that each variable-length structure should have a field in a well-known position (say offset zero) or use a special field name that is opaque to the DM application. For example, using the field name approach, the definition of the **dm_eventmsg_t** would be:

```
struct dm_eventmsg {
    ssize_t         _link;
    dm_type_t       ev_type;
    dm_token_t      ev_token;
    dm_vardata_t    ev_data;
};
```

The definition of the DM_STEP_TO_NEXT macro would then become:

```
#define DM_STEP_TO_NEXT(p, type) \
    ((type)((p)->_link ? (char *)(p) + (p)->_link : NULL))
```

6.11 Undeliverable Event Messages

The implementation of the DMAPI needs to specify the guidelines for delivery of a synchronous event message when no session exists to receive it. There are three choices with regard to synchronous event message delivery when no session exists:

- block the requesting process.
- return an error to the process that instigated the event.
- do not generate the event.

If an error is returned to the process, it may be specific to the operation that caused the event. This means that depending on the operation, two different errors can be returned for the same event type.

The implementation must also define the behavior for asynchronous events.

6.12 dm_vardata_t

One possible implementation of the **dm_vardata_t** structure is:

```
struct dm_vardata {
    ssize_t   vd_offset;
    size_t    vd_length;
};
typedef struct dm_vardata     dm_vardata_t;
```

where the offset field (*vd_offset*) in **dm_vardata_t** records the distance in bytes from the beginning of the structure in which the variable length data begins.

In the case of an event message, it records the beginning of the actual event-specific data. For other structures, such as **dm_stat_t**, it indicates where the handle data can be found. The definition of the two access macros would then be:

```
DM_GET_VALUE(p, field, type) \
            ((type)((char *)(p) + (p)->filed.vd_offset))

DM_GET_LEN(p, field)    ((p)->field.vd_length)
```

6.13 NFS Daemon Starvation

Special consideration needs to be taken when using DMAPI on a file system that is exported via NFS. Because a migrate-in operation can potentially take several seconds or even minutes, a large number of NFS client requests to files that are staged out could lead to NFS daemon starvation. Each NFS daemon could be waiting for a DMAPI operation to complete, with no free daemon threads left to accept new requests.

A possible solution to this problem is to devise a method for the file system to notify the NFS daemon when it detects that an operation will take an unusually long time. The NFS daemon could then fork a separate thread to wait for the migration to complete, and also send a EJUKEBOX notification to the client NFS.

The *dm_pending*( ) interface allows the DMAPI application to notify the DMAPI implementation if an operation is expected to be slow. The implementation may then take appropriate steps to notify NFS.

6.14 Unmount and Shutdown Deadlock

Unmount of a DMAPI managed File System can take a long time. This means the *shutdown* script needs to wait for the DM applications to finish with *unmount* activities before killing off processes. If *shutdown* kills the DM application process threads without first giving the DM application a chance to clean up its session IDs, then the *unmount* event will be posted to an orphan session and can never be responded to. *unmount* will then hang. However, if *shutdown* does not kill the non-DM application process threads, the File System may look busy forever, and *unmount* will likewise hang. *shutdown* therefore needs a way to kill all processes except the DM application processes.

6.15 The dt_change Field in dm_stat

The suggested implementation is to keep an in-kernel counter that is incremented every time it is read. In this way, released in-core inodes will be incrememted properly.

6.16 Punching Holes

If a call to *dm_punch_hole*( ) frees media resources, the DMAPI implementation should indicate these freed resources in subsequent calls to *dm_get_allocinfo*( ), by describing the freed extent with the DM_EXTENT_HOLE flag.

Glossary

DM application
A Data Management application is any application that uses the DMAPI.

DMAPI
Data Management Application Programming Interface. The term which refers to the interface defined by this XDSM Specification.

DMAPI implementation
The services in the host Operating System which act as the XDSM API provider

DMIG
Data Management Interfaces Group. This term refers to the group that developed this Data Storage Management interface interface between the UNIX kernel and data management applications.

event
A notification from the operating system kernel to a DM application about an operation on a file. For example, a DM application can arrange to be notified about attempts to read a particular file.

hole
An area of a file that consists entirely of bytes of zeros. Some file system implementations may not need to consume any media resources to maintain such an area.

managed file
A file that is being monitored by a DM application for events.

managed region
A contiguous span of a file given as an (offset, length) pair, together with an associated event generation specification.

multiple DM applications
In this document, the term multiple DM apps refers to multiple, non-cooperating and distinct applications that use the DMAPI. Note that a single product which happens to be constructed using multiple processes is not an example of "multiple DM applications", whereas something like a compression product from vendor A and a backup product from vendor B is.

operating system
In the context of the DMAPI, this is the code that includes the base kernel as well as any file system or extensions that may have been added to the kernel.

process
A single UNIX process. For purposes of this document, a process and a user thread are equivalent.

product
A specific DM application from a single vendor. A single product may consist of one or more processes working together.

token
A reference to state associated with a synchronous event message.

Index